Chicago's Grand
MIDWAY

publication supported by
Figure Foundation
rounding with the fairest

**UNIVERSITY OF
ILLINOIS PRESS**
Urbana, Chicago, and Springfield

Chicago's Grand MIDWAY

A Walk around the World at the Columbian Exposition

Norman Bolotin
with Christine Laing

Library of Congress Cataloging-in-Publication Data
Names: Bolotin, Norm, 1951– author. | Laing, Christine, co-author.
Title: Chicago's Grand Midway : a walk around the world at the
    Columbian Exposition / Norman Bolotin with Christine Laing.
Description: Urbana : University of Illinois Press, 2017. | Includes
    bibliographical references and index.
Identifiers: LCCN 2017007237 (print) | LCCN 2017010064 (ebook) |
    ISBN 9780252082429 (paperback) | ISBN 9780252099465 ()
Subjects: LCSH: World's Columbian Exposition (1893 : Chicago,
    Ill.)—History. | Midways—Illinois—Chicago—History—19th
    century. | Concessions (Amusements, etc.)—Illinois—
    Chicago—History—19th century. | Chicago (Ill.)—Social
    life and customs—19th century. | Chicago (Ill.)—Buildings,
    structures, etc. | BISAC: HISTORY / United States / State &
    Local / Midwest (IA, IL, IN, KS, MI, MN, MO, ND, NE, OH, SD,
    WI). | HISTORY / United States / 19th Century.
Classification: LCC T500.B2 B65 2017 (print) | LCC T500.B2
    (ebook) | DDC 791.06/80977311—dc23
LC record available at https://lccn.loc.gov/2017007237

Contents

Preface

One always encounters dead ends and pathways to nowhere in research. In more than thirty-five years of passionate pursuit of Columbian minutiae that might open new doors, I have often found road maps to such success. But in many cases it may have taken years or decades, not days or months.

My elation with such successes is generally tempered by the knowledge that whether it happens tomorrow or in another decade, additional information will eventually be uncovered that I will wish had been available for this book.

My first book, *Klondike Lost: A Decade of Photographs by Kinsey and Kinsey*, was published in 1980. I began researching the gold rush in 1976 and the Klondike gold rush town of Grand Forks a year later. Also known informally and in many government records as "Bonanza," the tent city grew into a boom town of ten thousand people in little more than a summer season of mining.

As soon as the gold was gone, so were all but a few hundred of the residents.

My reconstruction of life in the virtually unknown town in the Klondike River valley began with my own discovery of historical gold—several boxes of glass plate negatives of unpublished photos stored in the closet of the grandson of one of the photographers. It continued with the help of several gracious archivists, curators, and historians. But it succeeded because of the kindness of two women and one man who were three of the handful of children who had lived in the town for a few years spanning the nineteenth and twentieth centuries; when I interviewed them, they were in their late eighties and early nineties.

When those residents of the previously forgotten town passed away, despite archives of records and countless collections of documents, a deep hole appeared in the history of the gold rush. Nothing can replace the recollections of those who were there. With soft-spoken words, bright smiles, and the sparkling light from their reflected memories of childhood along Eldorado and Bonanza Creeks, they could make you feel that you had walked home with them from the tiny school, ankle-deep in mud along the streets where they sold papers, ran errands, and talked with the storekeepers, miners, Mounted Police, and even the "pretty ladies" (prostitutes).

Historians seldom count on having someone to interview personally. I was immensely fortunate to have had that window on the past, still in sharp focus, from articulate people who had experienced the Klondike gold rush as children. Having that luxury in the late 1970s did not just improve the 1980 book; it improved all of those I wrote after. It taught me to dig deeper, to seek diaries, to search incessantly for letters, notes, and documents that could make a story personal, not just historical.

I cannot articulate how much I wish I had discovered the World's Columbian Exposition just a few decades earlier, when I could have talked with those who rode the Ferris Wheel, waited tables at the Vienna Café, or operated— or rode on!—the Ice Railway. One can always find transcribed interviews and interpretations of what someone said in 1893, 1923, or 1943; but I savor those first-person naked thoughts, free of interpretation. Letters, diaries, and postcards give us human observations, but we cannot ask them for anything further: the color of a brocade, exactly what fearful meant, or precisely what one saw from atop the Ferris Wheel as it reached its arc.

In the case of the Midway, as a result of many personal delays (not the least of which was caring for my father for many years until his passing at the age of ninety-nine in 2014), I spent time I never would have had otherwise searching for postcards, letters, and perhaps another diary to build a more personal story. There is always a danger in considering century-old writings as factual, even when they are presented as such. And at the end of the Victorian era the norm was flowery, opinionated writing. I had to pore over every bit of material through an editorial filter and subject it to as many cross-referenced checks as humanly possible to verify facts, or to toss them out if they were not verifiable.

Still, despite Victorian journalists' propensity for opinionated writing and accepting (and thus presenting) the preposterous as facts, newspapers and other periodicals provided a wealth of excellent information—once you stripped away the superfluous and extracted the factual and valuable.

There can even be a danger in the seemingly unsullied. During my research I stumbled upon an interesting and unpublished several-page letter written by a woman who described her walk along the Midway in pleasant prose and seemingly accurate text. But in midstroll, the woman observed and shared her appreciation for a replica of the Leaning Tower of Pisa. Unfortunately, no tower modeled on the one in Pisa graced the Midway. I then had to question her other observations; perhaps she saw so much the day before writing the letter that the sights became a blur, or worse, she added secondhand details rather than religiously citing her own observations.

But how cold and academic would descriptions be if we simply saw the Midway in only metaphoric black and white? In 1893 photography was advanced to the point that we have a prodigious volume of photographs documenting the Midway—in black and white. Many writers gave us colorful accounts, while others were spare with their notes and impressions. We also were fortunate that a handful of artists gave us literal color to complement what was often more figurative in fairgoers' writings. One of the most prolific among the artists was watercolorist Charles Graham, whose work is featured in the color plates. His paintings of the fair were published in numerous books, exhibitor pamphlets, the Chicago Tribune, and various published portfolios. Without his work, the radiance of a literal rainbow of colors from exhibitors around the world and the sharp contrast between the Midway and the "White City" of the main grounds would have been conspicuously absent in both our impressions and our understanding of the fair. Time and time again, the first-person accounts and impressions of the Midway focus on the array of skin colors, colorful clothing, unfamiliar musical instruments, languages, and foods from around the globe. For the vast majority of visitors to the fair, the Midway was their introduction to a non-Western world.

Born to Study World's Fairs

As a child of seven in 1958, reading the daily newspaper one day (which I did routinely if not perspicaciously) I discovered that there was a world's fair under way that very year. I imagined, from the scant amount I had read, that a world's fair was not unlike Disneyland I had already visited. That year's fair was being held in Brussels, Belgium, and I immediately beseeched my parents to take the family. My parents both looked down into my excited eyes with that blank stare of confusion parents often seemed to have.

They asked me for an explanation and offered me an adult reality. I had confused Belgium with Bellingham, a city one hundred miles north of our Seattle home. As bright and creative as youngsters can be, they often fall victim to a simple lack of worldly information or complex vocabulary. It wouldn't be my last error of this type. I was confused and failed to comprehend just why we were not able to drive to Belgium some afternoon.

Just two years later I was officially imbued with what even a not-quite-ten-year-old understood. Seattle's first world's fair since 1909 was under construction and infusing the city with excitement. This one would be much closer than Brussels or even Bellingham.

One day some mail arrived addressed to me from the Century 21 Exposition. It included a color brochure and a letter noting that someone was very happy to hear of my interest in the forthcoming fair. Over the next several months

there were decals, bumper stickers, first-day stamped envelopes, pins, and lots of literature arriving in our mail, all addressed to me, and all of which went into a box of treasures along with clippings from the evening paper. My mother, a veteran of Little League, PTA, and Cub Scouts before it was fashionable, also worked full-time and had begun accumulating anything related to the fair for me. She also ensured that my name was on more than a few mailing lists promoting the Century 21 Exposition.

As the world's fair drew closer, its most noticeable feature grew taller by the week. The Space Needle (which I could see from my bedroom window by the time it was about three quarters finished) began hosting visitors weeks before opening day, giving them a unique look down on exhibit buildings under construction. Of course my parents took my sister and me for that prefatory look—and the sight of those unfinished pavilions as the elevator took us to the top of the Needle is still etched in my mind as my favorite view of the world's fair more than half a century later.

Just before the official opening in April 1962, my father, a machinist, accepted a job for the six-month run of the fair as the one-man machine shop tasked to repair or replace anything that cracked, stuck, or otherwise malfunctioned at the Seattle World's Fair, day or night. Needless to say, I was ecstatic and didn't fail to share the important news with neighbors and classmates.

My family went to the fair numerous times, and I quickly learned the precise location of every arcade and every exhibit of interest (to me)—the Boeing Spacearium, the city of the future in the World of Century 21, the Skyride, and of course the Space Needle—along with every souvenir stand that awaited my hoarded allowance money. When out-of-town guests visited, I begged to be their tour guide.

But it was my dad who opened the portal to what no other children would experience. None. Even the children of the fair's president, who could meet celebrities, enter for free, or go to the front of any line, never roamed the still, empty grounds with their father in the middle of the night. Whenever I was at the fair with my mother and sister, out-of-town relatives, or just local friends, my father told me to watch the clock, and when the fair closed at 10 p.m. to clandestinely drift over to the basement of the Food Circus (a large building with every imaginable culinary and high-calorie delight) to the door of the machine shop. I was terrified that security guards might see me moving counter to the crowds and demand an explanation; in reality, none of them ever did, and had they seen me moving with purpose they probably would have ignored me altogether.

I entered the mechanical Land of Oz—drill press, lathe, pipe cutter, all neatly arranged in a compact setting—a machine shop with just enough room for one man and enough equipment for half a dozen specialists—or one expert in them all. As long as they had a journeyman who could operate every machine and who was an expert at jury-rigging a bolt, hook, or clamp, fair management was happy to outfit the shop and employ a single machinist to manage it.

I would sit and study the shop's array of equipment until the fairgrounds had completely emptied. My dad and I then hopped into a little vehicle much like a golf cart (but with a pickup bed where I rode, imagining I was the crown prince of fairdom) and emerged into the quiet darkness lit by minimal lights rather than the explosion of daytime colors and flashing neon. The fair was mine. We would stop at the monorail to pick up a piece of the copper-topped steel power rail that provided electricity to the train, at a gate with a jammed turnstile, or to repair something as mundane as a broken hinge on a door.

I knew more about the Seattle World's Fair, I'm sure, than almost any ten-year-old; and over the years, I never stopped feeding my insatiable desire for stories, little-known facts, and endless details about the fair. I began my research and collecting in rather pedestrian fashion: I scoured the grounds for dropped ticket stubs or other interesting-looking papers both during daytime visits and during those nighttime sojourns.

By 1962 I was already an inveterate collector of the "normal" kid stuff—such as baseball and football cards—supplemented by anything related to the world's fair. In 1979, as an adult, at a local coin show I stumbled on a beautiful prooflike medal from the World's Columbian Exposition. The medal, still in its original box of issue, was inexpensive and wanting for a home. I spent the next decade researching and collecting most anything from the World's Columbian Exposition. I decided I wanted to write a history of the fair. By this time I'd written my second history of the Klondike gold rush and a Civil War history and had edited and published a Holocaust diary. I began shopping my idea for a history of the fair and had no takers until the National Trust for Historic Preservation asked me to write it in 1991. I shifted from low into overdrive to complete my research and write the book to meet a deadline for publication during the 1993 centennial of the fair.

For that history, I supplemented traditional research by purchasing every book, pamphlet, and directory from the fair that I could find. I exploited all my knowledge as a writer/historian and collector to build my own Columbian library and file of information. I used public and private archives, other collectors' files, and a variety of auctions to collect data. I continued collecting after the first book was published and have not stopped through the completion of this book.

After the first book was published, through the end of the 1990s, I taught a summer course for museum and book publishing editors at the University of Chicago. One day I found a few minutes to escape the frenetic pace for a moment's solitude outside. Had I smoked this would have been one of those self-defining breaks—"I'll just grab a cigarette and be right back"—but since I didn't, I sat on the concrete steps of the university building looking across 59th Street at the Midway Plaisance. There was just enough noise to catch my attention, including bits of music and the sound of a voice on a bullhorn thanking the quickly disappearing audience for coming. Ingenious tents were folded away, plastic bins and coolers were loaded, and individual chairs and tables were neatly packed into carrying cases light enough to fling over the shoulder.

I had no idea who the people were or what the group was undertaking across from the University of Chicago building.

It was still sunny and a welcome, almost cool breeze came from Lake Michigan to the east. On the grassy expanse of the Midway, black men and women in brightly colored attire were dismantling their weekend cultural event. I only caught flashes of dazzling colors and had no idea if the event were African or perhaps Caribbean. Much like the Midway of a century earlier, delicious scents, colorful clothing, and unfamiliar voices melded into a collage in which one could revel even if unsure of the contents.

I drank in the final notes of music and the clatter of packing. The voices were loud enough to hear but distant enough to be indistinguishable. The hugs and handshakes all seemed to be accompanied by broad smiles. I briefly closed my eyes and absorbed the overlapping sounds. As I leaned back and gazed peacefully, I imagined that the tent being taken down was part of the German Village that once sat across 59th. The enormous shadow of the Ferris Wheel engulfed the German Village and cast a grayness over the bright sunshine on the Java Village and the thousands of visitors walking along the crowded Midway.

In my imagination, new, crisp voices seeped out from each corner, from the backs of buildings I could see around and through. Women fanned themselves with hats and papers as they walked along in their native attire draped loosely around their bodies, exposing nothing but arms to the afternoon sun. Male Columbian exhibitors from Europe suffered in tight-collared shirts and jackets; their counterparts

from Asia and Africa were more comfortable in looser–fitting, scanter clothing. Male fairgoers carried coats on their arms but still sported ties and starched, upturned collars; regardless of attire, performers were exhausted from a dozen hours on their feet in one of the hottest Chicago summers on record. Virtually all the tourists battled the bright light and heat with bowlers or umbrellas. Hawkers from around the globe sold rugs, souvenirs, jewelry, and refreshing drinks. The backs of clapboard buildings and the high fence facing north were nondescript, but flags and pennants and the giant blue dome of the Moorish Palace on the south side of the Plaisance dominated my view.

I gazed from side to side and tried to pull in familiar words or dialects, something discernible. I strained to absorb more, and my visual and aural filters gathered in the Arabic, Turkish, German, Dutch, and smatterings of English. Beyond, the center of the Midway was like a Charles Graham watercolor. I saw a sudden stillness as the chaos became a three-dimensional, mile-long work of art.

I vaguely heard a voice, "Norm . . . Norm; we're ready to get started again." An assistant was patting my shoulder and interrupting my travel. I was short of breath as I blinked and slipped uncomfortably, more disappointed than I could explain, back to the concrete stairs where I sat, back to the present. I arose slowly and wandered down the hall to a small classroom of adult students.

I walked up to the podium, scanned the room full of faces, and turned to look out the window on 59th Street. The Midway Plaisance was empty but for a few young men playing baseball and parents flying kites with their children. From my vantage point I couldn't see either the east or west end of the Plaisance, but it was a peaceful, quiet parkway, as it was for most of the nineteenth century and all of the twentieth. I refocused my attention for a lecture on the profitability of book publishing based on production variables.

I wondered to myself if in 1893 the Java Village and Cairo Street business managers calculated the unit cost or potential profit of their concessions' guide booklets; many of the latter were full of color artwork and were remarkably professional and attractive.

Teaching a course that looks out on the Midway Plaisance, an unassuming lawn awaiting a picnic or a game of touch football, was like drinking in a historical aphrodisiac.

East, beyond the end of the Midway, is the Museum of Science and Industry, originally the Palace of Fine Arts of the World's Columbian Exposition. The dirty, swamplike lagoon that reaches to the museum's original south stairs was once a piece of the Frederick Law Olmsted's Venice-like waterways surrounding Wooded Island, which remains but is now dark and dingy and unsafe to wander alone after dark.

A treasure hunter's dream of picking up a ticket stub to the Ferris Wheel or an 1893 penny dropped unnoticed is futile; and even though the waters of the remaining bit of lagoon are shallow, visibility is nonexistent. Long overdue, college archaeology programs have recently conducted digs in the area, finding treasures that appeal only to scientists and historians. It seems the real treasures surface in antique shops, at estate sales, at flea markets, and, of course, on eBay these days.

Spending little bits of my summers so close to the Midway was like a wondrous infection that crawled slowly under my skin and into my senses. Every day that passes makes it more indelible, a more permanent part of my own past and memory.

I walk along the streets adjacent and perpendicular to the Midway, on the sidewalk across the boulevard where the university buildings all face history. It is relatively easy, despite the architecture, to tell which university buildings were constructed in 1892 or 1893 as opposed to decades later. They're all connected by an invisible lifeline that binds them together, me to them, and both of us to the Midway Plaisance. The overpasses no longer look down on hundreds of thousands of people strolling between the main fairgrounds and the Midway. Nowadays, modern locomotives slow as they pass the Midway, and instead of carriages, cars continue unabated and unaware as they pass this history separated by a lush green lawn.

The Midway Plaisance, a simple parkway a single mile long, is a Möbius strip of history that wraps itself around early Chicago, through its own metamorphosis to the world's first midway, and back again to the becalmed boulevard, home to ballgames, picnics, and couples strolling hand in hand.

Norman Bolotin
Woodinville, Washington

Acknowledgments

There are always far too many people to acknowledge in the writing of a book, from those who helped in the protracted research to those of infinite value answering queries, verifying facts, and finally editing and publishing the work.

This book is the result of more than three decades of research that began well before publication of our first book about the fair, *The World's Columbian Exposition: The Chicago World's Fair of 1893*, the first edition of which coincided with the exposition's centennial in 1993. I am sure I have forgotten many people who were integral to the process many years ago. To each of you, I apologize for not acknowledging you individually.

Without the foresight and patience of one individual, our first history of the fair would not still be in print, I am quite sure, nor would this new book about the Midway Plaisance have ever come to fruition. Willis "Bill" Regier, recently retired as this book goes to press, was for many years director of the University of Illinois Press and its guiding light. He stepped in when the National Trust ended its book publishing operation that had been so vital to the historical community. It was the Trust, and its Preservation Press, that published the centennial history I coauthored with my wife and business partner, Christine Laing. Sandra Harner, art director, colleague, and a friend for more than forty years, designed a beautiful leather slipcased limited edition for Trust members and a hardcover trade edition of the book.

As that hardcover edition sold out, I had no illusions of seeing the book republished in softcover. But Bill saw the need and market for it. I learned long ago in publishing that good books can die without a champion in the right place. Bill and the Press rescued our history of the fair, and it has been in print in softcover for nearly twenty years. I am deeply indebted to him for publishing that book, and even more for his support when I proposed this book . . .

and his understanding through innumerable delays in bringing it to fruition. Many, if not most, publishers would not have waited so long for me to complete this project.

When Bill retired, press editor Danny Nasset stepped in to work with me and guide the book through its final development. Danny made the transition seamless, was a pleasure to work with, and ensured that the high standards we all had were met.

Throughout the publishing process, many players are typically hidden from the public, but their efforts add a great deal to a book. I had the pleasure of working with numerous members of the press staff: Jennifer Comeau, assistant press director and project editor, massaged and repaired my usage, consistency and style errors, and foibles; Dustin Hubbart, art director, was responsible for creating the first thing the public sees (the cover!) and for overseeing Jim Proefrock's design and layout of the interior; Kristine Ding ensured high-quality printing; Michael Roux, Steve Fast, Kevin Cunningham, and Heather Gernenz were—and continue to be—tasked with marketing, selling, and promoting the finished product; and further behind the scenes, Roberta Sparenberg and Marika Christofides were patient and pleasant in extracting the smallest bits of information from me, again, to ensure the quality of the book.

Two individuals were absolutely critical to my research on the first book. Much of what I found with their expert assistance was beyond the scope of the first book and invaluable to the second. Mary Woolever of the Art Institute of Chicago helped me unearth original fair documents and reports, including president Harlow Higinbotham's final report and other documents from his tenure at the exposition's helm.

Andrea Mark Telli was an archivist in Special Collections at the Chicago Public Library when she first threw open the library's expansive historical files for me in 1991, and she continued to act as my personal "historical doctor" on call, always accessible and inestimably helpful over the years with my research for both

Columbian books and also several Civil War histories. She has suffered that inevitable fate of being "kicked upstairs" in Chicago's library system, an unfortunate loss for those myriad researchers using the outstanding public archives, but I'm sure an extraordinary addition to the management of the city's library system and the needs of Chicagoans.

On another level of the research process are collectors who are often discounted as amateur historians, allegedly lacking sophistication, breadth of knowledge, and understanding of nuances and intimate details of history surrounding their collections. Nothing could be further from the truth. In articles I've written over the years about the concept of the collector as curator, I have repeatedly seen that some of the most important and insightful research on numerous subjects has come from those whose passion encompasses not only a physical collection but also the knowledge built over years of collecting.

The collecting expertise of and research by several individuals were especially helpful to me over many years in this book's development. John Kennel, already a longtime collector and student of the World's Columbian Exposition when I first discovered it, was always gracious in answering questions or discussing a dilemma I had encountered. I vividly recall being delighted, finally, to have the opportunity to reciprocate for all of his help when he asked me an obscure Midway question. John passed away in 2014, leaving a palpable void in the World's Columbian Exposition community. I was about to contact him yet again with a question only he could answer when his wife, Heike, informed me of his passing. She, too, over many years, has generously shared her knowledge of the fair. David Flippin and I shared a passion for exposition history and a relatively narrow field of collecting original Columbian literature and documents. For many years he and I communicated frequently about such esoteric items as a Cairo Street brochure (plate 1), a "vertical transit" (elevator) ticket, and passes to allow important guests through Chicago police lines during the fair's dedication. David has always been a calm, sophisticated, intelligent collector and researcher, and when he decided to sell his Columbian collection and refocus on collecting fine antiques I was terribly—and selfishly—disappointed to lose an active colleague as passionate about the world's fair as I am. David and John were of far more value, substantively and psychologically, to me over the years than either knew.

Many other Columbian collectors (far too many to name) have, over several decades of passionate exchanges, led me down productive roads—and detours!—that many historians would miss or discount. For example, one long-time collector, James Morgan, shares my tenacity for pursuing seemingly trivial details. He has been relentless in unearthing details regarding World's Columbian Exposition attendance and specialty tickets to the fair.

I am grateful to Gerald Danzer, professor emeritus at the University of Illinois at Chicago, for his astute review of the final manuscript for this book.

Finally, I would be remiss in not thanking my family for their unflagging support, despite my sharing far more about Columbiana than any of them has a desire to hear. Christine Laing, my partner in life and business, has coauthored and developed numerous books with me, and once again she was available to provide critical review, assistance, and moral support as the deadline approached. Our children—Jacob, Zack, and Hannah—have shared opinions on the book and listened to years of anxiety about it, and throughout they have been wonderfully supportive.

xix

Chicago's Grand
MIDWAY

Creating the World's First Midway

The first world's fair was held in London in 1851, but the history of exhibitions and expositions is far longer than the short span of time between that first world's fair and the World's Columbian Exposition. The centuries of local and regional fairs that preceded the first world's fair were relevant to it in an evolutionary sense, but once they morphed into actual "world's" fairs, the content and scope grew exponentially. By the time the World's Columbian Exposition was held, the acceleration of change and evolution was dramatic.

Fairs have been held to introduce societies to new inventions and new interpretations of civilization. As cities and countries grew, industry evolved, and societies changed, fairs' presentations were a direct result of that societal progress and also of mankind's unceasing desire to capture the past and project the future.

The World's Columbian Exposition owes its existence, at least in the abstract, to literal lawn parties of medieval English royalty. Those earliest fairs a thousand years ago often were held under the auspices of the English Crown, as a gift to paupers, farmers, and members of uneducated classes. They celebrated a military victory or helped restore morale on the heels of a drought or military defeat. The Crown bestowed its blessing on the event for its illiterate class, but the much smaller monarchical upper class enjoyed the spoils. None of the "unwashed" class attending the brief celebrations complained of inequity because for a single moment in their lives, the peasants enjoyed a break in the monotony and struggles of their meager existence. They could be physically close to royalty and overlords without fearing malevolence.

For the royalty and its court, there were social events—banquets and balls and the sporting combat of swordsmen and jousters—along with minstrels, jugglers, and magicians. It was the closest the upper and lower classes ever came to commingling. For a very brief time, all the English men, women, and children were ersatz equals.

These nameless fairs, visual benchmarks of the medieval era, have been backdrops of innumerable films about the period. They showed the different classes and represented the progress of people and civilization. Since 1851, world's fairs likewise have symbolized humanity's best foot forward.

It's not surprising that as Western Europe evolved, so did fairs and exhibitions. As literacy increased, so did the frequency of fairs. By the seventeenth and eighteenth centuries, major European cities held exhibitions and expositions worthy of historical note, although closer in size to those of a thousand years earlier than to those of a few decades later. The Industrial Revolution saw the advent of industrial fairs, bringing the era's technological advancements to the public. London, Liverpool, Brussels, and Paris all sponsored events that drew attendance from across national borders.

These were the forebears of the World's Columbian Exposition. The planning commissions of each fair studied the successes and failures of those immediately preceding it.

Queen Victoria gave us a name for the era of her sixty-one years on the throne. It was her consort, Prince Albert, who took fairs to an entirely new level in both content and size with the first exposition dubbed a "world's" fair. Albert was intimately involved in social and educational activities in England after he and Victoria married. Victoria often ceded political and royal tasks to him. The English people were initially wary of Victoria's German cousin when they married, but he rapidly won over the country with his dedication to Victoria and to England, as well as to its growth and development.

As nineteenth-century fairs blossomed, many were international and could easily have launched the term "worlds' fair." Between 1830 and 1850 Paris hosted five expositions/fairs; Turin, Italy, hosted eight; and Great Britain was the site of two. The only reason none were called "world's fairs" was simply that no one had coined the phrase. Albert was responsible for the moniker and the exposition that became the

line of demarcation between centuries of small and local fairs and the age of world's fairs.

Prince Albert oversaw the planning, management, and construction of the 1851 fair in London's Hyde Park. The exposition was larger than any previous fair by a prodigious magnitude. Albert's goal was to expand the reach of England's industrial, commercial, and transportation industries—and demonstrate their superiority. The plan called for the venue to be an exhibition in itself. The first Crystal Palace was all that, and more.

The architectural design and construction of the cast-iron and plate-glass Crystal Palace was unique at the time. Most fairs and expositions had been held in existing facilities or in new ones similar to existing structures. The Crystal Palace was 1,848 feet long and 456 feet wide and used 1.25 million square feet of glass. Albert not only invited individuals and businesses from all over Europe, unlike the status quo of industrial expositions focused solely on western European nations, but he also courted business and political leaders of two geographically distant countries, India and the United States. Relatively few countries had recognized the growth and economic potential of the United States, with much of England still regarding the country as little more than a former colony. Dealing with America and American business still required a long voyage across the Atlantic, and for U.S. companies to exhibit at or attend the 1851 world's fair in London required a massive commitment of time and money.

The exposition was formally called the Great Exhibition of the Works of Industry of All Nations. A newspaper writer in England dubbed the new fair "Prince Albert's *World's* Fair." From that point forward the name was a part of our vocabulary. All fairs have been inexorably linked to the evolution of our societies and their arts and industries, but Prince Albert made arguably the greatest single leap forward of any fair before or after.

Prince Albert's ambitious plan for filling the Crystal Palace called for fourteen thousand exhibitors and some one hundred thousand objects on display. It was a huge success by every measure, from the structure to the breadth of participants. Despite the fact that travel of any distance was slow and difficult, the attendance at the first world's fair was a rather astounding six million.

Since 1851, more than two hundred international expositions, exhibits, fairs, and world's fairs have been held. Some were of the magnitude of the World's Columbian Exposition, and some were smaller in focus or created with dramatically different expectations—in attendance and revenue. Success, financial and otherwise, has come with attendance of less than one million and more than fifty million.

Other fairs have drawn relatively large attendance numbers but, for a variety of reasons, failed to be profitable.

The World's Columbian Exposition

The World's Columbian Exposition of 1893 was the first world's fair to separate itself into two distinct components, but it took management of the fair virtually the entire planning period to decide just how to present the world's first midway.

The Midway Plaisance was to be a part of the fairgrounds from the earliest days of planning, as the mile-long boulevard perpendicular to the more than six-hundred-acre main site seemed a

Some of the finest views (this one to the west) of the fairgrounds were from atop the tallest buildings. There were elevators to take guests to a viewing balcony on the Manufactures and Liberal Arts Building. The pathways and lagoon in the foreground lead to the Horticulture Building, the dominant feature of the photograph even though only a little more than half of the structure is shown. To the right is the Woman's Building, and between and just behind the two buildings, difficult to discern due to the angle, begins the Midway. Hyde Park construction surrounds the area, including numerous hotels and the newly opened University of Chicago campus.

logical supplement to the main grounds. How to incorporate it was a far more difficult decision. The Grand Buildings, expansive waterways, foreign and state buildings, and specialty structures forming the White City progressed at breakneck speed. The Midway, on the other hand, was slow to coalesce.

The formal planning process began just four years before the target opening when Congress passed "A Bill To Provide for a Permanent Exposition of the Three Americas at the National capital in Honor of the Four Hundredth Anniversary of the Discovery of America."

At the same time, construction of the 1889 Exposition Universelle in Paris, the largest world's fair ever held, was under way. The City of Lights had already hosted three of the great world's fairs of the century in 1855, 1867, and 1878. The fourth was the most dramatic, featuring construction of the Eiffel Tower. U.S. Congressional leaders were well aware of the 1889 Paris exposition when they began to debate the issue of a major exposition in the United States for 1892.

Four cities submitted serious proposals—St. Louis, New York, Chicago, and Washington, DC. The debates and proposals were protracted and antagonistic. Washington and St. Louis were eliminated relatively quickly in the process, leaving an unexpected and anomalous head-to-head competition between favored New York and "upstart" Chicago.

New York leaders cited their vast experience with major events, including the country's first world's fair in 1853 (although it received little recognition outside the country), its status as the largest city in the country in every census taken, and its major port facilities serving Europe, the eastern seaboard, and the West. It also had enormous private capital resources.

Chicago had a long list of attributes that ultimately made it the better choice for the fair site. It had a thriving business community and was blessed with two thousand acres of parks, including expansive areas of Lake Michigan waterfront. Nearly half the acreage was in Jackson

Attendance at Nineteenth-Century World's Fairs*	
Year, City	Estimated Attendance (rounded to the nearest million)
1851, London	6.0 million
1853, New York	1.0 million
1855, Paris	5.0 million
1862, London	2.0 million
1867, Paris	7.0 million
1873, Vienna	7.0 million
1876, Philadelphia	10.0 million
1878, Paris	16.0 million
1889, Paris	28.0 million*
1893, Chicago	28.0 million*

* Each fair measured its attendance somewhat differently, depending on complimentary passes, employees using turnstiles when coming to work, etc. The World's Columbian Exposition figure of 28 million included some 7 million unpaid visits. Paris's net paid attendance in 1889 was estimated at 25 million versus 28.1 million total.

and Washington Parks, with the Midway Plaisance between. Further, twenty-four railroads had terminals in Chicago, creating an elaborate and highly efficient network for transporting people and freight. Exhibitors and vendors would present massive freight requirements in both volume and speed, and the Chicago delegation cited its capability to deliver both—as well as millions of visitors.

Reportedly the city's steam railroads, steamboats, and excursion boats combined could carry more than two million passengers per eighteen-hour day.

Chicago also made its bid on the basis of its central location, wealth, and enterprises, as well as its status as one of the fastest-growing cities in the world, both before and after the Great Fire of 1871. In the census of 1870, Chicago was the fifth largest city in the United States with a

The cover of New York's proposal to Congress for the right to host the world's fair celebrating the four-hundredth anniversary of Columbus's "discovery" of America reads more like the preface—150 words to announce its intentions!

population of 298,977, compared to New York's 942,292. One would have expected a decline in Chicago's population with the devastation of the fire, yet the census of 1880 showed that Chicago had grown to half a million—while New York became the first city in the country with more than a million residents (1.2 million). By 1890, as Congress was debating the concept and scope of the world's fair as well as its location, Chicago had become the second largest city in the United States with a population of 1.1 million compared to New York's 1.5 million.

The size of the host city had effectively been eliminated as a factor in the decision. While Chicago was not on the ocean, it was adjacent to 22,000-square-mile Lake Michigan, and fair proponents described their plans to construct the fairgrounds—with a theme of water throughout—at Jackson Park along the shores of Lake Michigan.

Members of New York's delegation beseeched Congress to consider the fact that it made no sense to hold a world's fair celebrating Columbus's voyage of discovery in the center of the country. How could congress *not* select New York and the Atlantic Ocean?

On February 25, 1890, Congress shocked New York by selecting Chicago to host the greatest fair the country had ever seen, and arguably one to challenge the Paris spectacle that had just closed.

Chicago faced an arduous landscape and construction task, not to mention securing foreign and domestic public and private participants with just thirty months to go until the original congressional goal of opening on Columbus Day 1892.

Although many observers cited what they believed to be Chicago's failure to meet the deadline, any idea of reaching that goal had already been abandoned by the time the city was selected. Instead, the buildings and grounds would be dedicated in October 1892, and the actual opening of the fair would be six months later.

At this stage the Midway Plaisance as a part of the exposition was no more than a lovely boulevard adjacent to the main grounds. It was deemed a logical bit of land to add to the grounds of Jackson Park, but no one was quite sure how to use it as a complement to or a piece of the main fairgrounds.

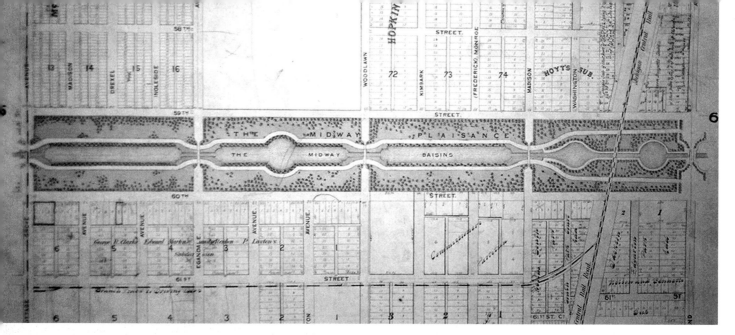

This plan of waterways in and through the Midway was published in 1876 as part of a large atlas by Chicago map company Horace and Greeley, which noted that the details for this map were obtained "from public records and private surveys." Though he is not credited, the map had to have originated with plans that Frederick Law Olmsted, already the preeminent landscape architect in America when the atlas was published, created before the Chicago Fire of 1871, and before he realized that his design was unworkable. More than two decades later Olmsted returned to Chicago to create the landscape masterpiece that is arguably the most spectacular ever created for a world's fair. Historians have discussed these early Midway plans for more than a century, but only recently was this illustration discovered. Map courtesy of James Leach of jimsoldmaps, South Bend, Indiana.

Early morning was the best time for official photographers to obtain static photos of the grounds highlighting the waterways, main buildings, and statuary. C. D. Arnold, the official photographer, spent many hours over the weeks illustrating every landscape and architectural feature, and then repeating the process photographing the tens of thousands of people who could be seen at any time the fair was open in most any fair location. This picture looks south over the canal and bridges; the Manufactures and Liberal Arts Building, with its sloped, low, and long domed roof, is instantly recognizable.

This picture looks south toward the Peristyle; in the foreground, the fountain and statue of Columbia seems like a collection of dancing mermaids. The size of the various interconnected lagoons and canals can be deceiving depending on the view. Occasionally, a close-up photo across a waterway, dwarfed by the surrounding buildings, gives an impression of a narrow and inconsequential body of water. Here, electric launches and gondolas appear no more than tiny toys in the distance, and this one of many "ponds" appears anything but tiny.

One of the most magnificent views of the main grounds was from the roof of the Manufactures and Liberal Arts Building. Note the large searchlight, one of many used to light the grounds after dark. Visitors could pay to take a modern Victorian contrivance to the rooftop—an elevator! This woman is probably a visitor, while the two Columbian guards were likely stationed on the roof to ensure that no one fell or jumped. The massive building across from the Manufactures and Liberal Arts Building is Machinery Hall.

The Midway Plaisance existed long before Chicago had any thought of hosting a fair. Hyde Park developer Paul Cornell had retained Frederick Law Olmsted, the acknowledged father of American landscape architecture, to develop plans for Washington Park and to consider creating a canal between Washington and Jackson Parks. The canal never came to fruition due to the water table and the relative elevations of the park and Lake Michigan—any such canal would have continually drained into the lake. These plans were developed more than two decades before construction on the fair began. Cornell envisioned the Plaisance as a centerpiece of a new community that would be home to a university and summer retreats for wealthy Chicagoans.

The Great Fire in 1871 put Cornell's plans on hold, and the Plaisance remained a tree-lined boulevard. By the time the University of Chicago opened it was 1892 and Olmsted was designing the Venetian waterways of the fairgrounds. He developed ambitious and creative ideas to cut, slice, and rearrange the dirt and swamp of Jackson Park into what was arguably the most beautiful world's fair site of the nineteenth—or any—century. Through it all, the Midway was the subject of much talk and virtually no action.

The Midway was a mile-long arrow pointing to the east and the main fairgrounds—to the Woman's and Horticulture Buildings at the west edge of the grounds, and on to the main lagoon, Wooded Island, Fisheries Building, and Lake Michigan.

As construction of the fair moved ahead at a hectic pace, the first idea, never fully developed, of how to incorporate the Midway was to lead fairgoers along an ethnographic journey of human evolution as they walked its length to the main grounds. Ethnography was a new scientific discipline, and its preeminent scholar was on the fair's staff. Frederick Putnam, the director of Harvard's Peabody Museum of Archaeology and Ethnology, had been appointed the fair's head of anthropology in January 1891.

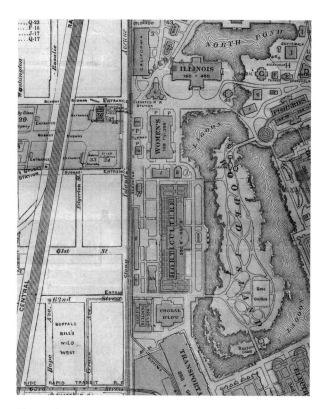

Horticulture and Woman's Buildings and the east end of the Midway abutting the main fairgrounds.

A condition of his taking the job was that the fair would provide him an ample budget to send crews around the world to collect specimens for display. With the benefit of hindsight, Putnam's and early science's rampage through villages and sacred sites around the globe has been justifiably criticized. However, exposition scientific teams did operate under strict guidelines developed for these early anthropologists and ethnologists. The fair developed comprehensive guidelines not only for the handling, labeling, shipping, and display of artifacts but for the conscientious gathering of specimens and respectful treatment of indigenous peoples and their lands. While the crews' excavation and other processes were not nearly as sophisticated as contemporary work, they paid unusually close attention to any disturbances of the cultures they sought to display.

Thankfully, the early plan for the Midway related to Putnam's ethnographic work was never realized. It called for visitors entering

8

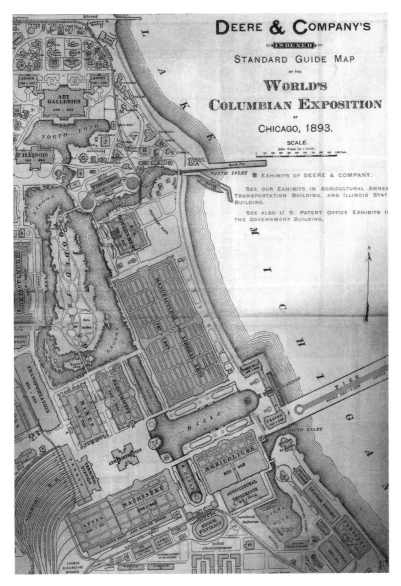

The main grounds.

Map text:

DEERE & COMPANY'S

INDEXED

STANDARD GUIDE MAP

OF THE

WORLD'S

COLUMBIAN EXPOSITION

AT

CHICAGO, 1893.

SCALE.

EXHIBITS OF DEERE & COMPANY.

SEE OUR EXHIBITS IN AGRICULTURAL ANNEX TRANSPORTATION BUILDING, AND ILLINOIS STATE BUILDING.

SEE ALSO U. S. PATENT OFFICE EXHIBITS IN THE GOVERNMENT BUILDING.

harshly as those fairs who presented "human zoos" of Africans and others. Fortunately for those who visited the World's Columbian Exposition, Putnam was too busy to become involved in creating such an exhibit, and instead a young entrepreneur named Sol Bloom rescued the Midway.

Creating the Midway

While the Columbian Exposition's main grounds and buildings were taking shape at a dizzying pace, fair management continued to struggle with just how to incorporate the Midway into the fair.

Chicago was not the first world's fair to feature sociocultural exhibits, but no other had conceived of a separate section of the fair focused on aboriginal peoples or entertainment as its own distinct section of a world's fair.

The 1878 Paris exposition, like all of that city's great fairs, was held in the center of the city along the Seine River, winding through and encompassing the existing downtown like a grand prix race course. That fair was the first to feature a "Human Zoo of Indigenous People." It was the first attempt at presenting other cultures from various parts of the world at the world's fair.

Paris's 1889 world's fair featured expanded cultural exhibits and concessions scattered about the grounds. These included the Vietnam Actor's Theater, Street in Cairo, Java Village, and Algerian Village, as well as the French Colonial Exhibit. Each was integrated into the fairgrounds and presented in the same way as any other exhibit, interspersed with art, architecture, technology, transportation, and other features.

from the west to walk along a human evolution exhibit from one end of the Midway to the other. They would then enter the main grounds having seen the white Western human at the top of this evolutionary ladder. It was unclear who championed this idea, but the legacy of the fair would have suffered had it been undertaken. The nebulous idea as discussed among fair directors showed early man likened to other primates and moving through the ages, with the height of evolution being—of course—the civilized white man. History likely would have judged the fair and its Midway Plaisance as

These long houses, totems, and canoes from the Pacific Northwest (U.S. and Canadian) were at the southeast corner of the main grounds, under Putnam's purview.

Harlow N. Higinbotham, a well-respected Chicago civic and business leader and president of the exposition corporation, had dozens of important tasks on his desk, but the difficult question of what to do with the Midway lingered on.

It was certainly serendipitous that Sol Bloom had visited the 1889 world's fair and struck up a working relationship with the Algerian performers in Paris. He arranged to serve as their manager and coordinate their village/building in Chicago. When he inquired about location and learned about the indistinct status of the Midway, he met with Higinbotham and convinced him not only of his savvy in marketing but his understanding of how to create an enticing and professional Midway, developing it into a cohesive international exhibition and entertainment center for the fair. It had languished a ridiculously long time, and the opening was dangerously near. Hiring Bloom (just

twenty-three years old when the fair opened) to manage the Midway was a huge risk but one that Higinbotham felt he had to take with no other options on the horizon.

To develop and manage the Midway, Bloom was paid a more-than-princely salary by nineteenth-century standards of one thousand dollars per week from the time he started developing the Midway through the end of the six-month world's fair.

Higinbotham also formed a new department, the Section of Isolated Exhibits, with John Bidlake of North Dakota appointed as superintendent. Bidlake's job was mostly political, while Bloom was responsible for management and marketing of the Midway. Bidlake's corporate duties included oversight of such exhibits as the Esquimaux Village and Cliff Dwellers' Exhibit, both of which were on the main grounds, and "the various villages of the native peoples on the Plaisance [who] were of much interest from their faithful representation of native life and customs in distant countries." That such exhibits as those of the Esquimaux and Cliff Dwellers were part of the fair—on the main grounds, not the Midway—posed a level of concern for fair management and confusion for many fairgoers. But such contradictions in concession placement ended up being of very minor consequence once the exposition opened.

Bloom was the antithesis of the professorial Putnam and the public servants overseeing the fair. But he did not disappoint.

The Algerian troupe arrived early, unaware that the fair opened in 1893 rather than 1892—although in some of the oft-misguided papers of the era, they were said to have arrived late! Bloom housed his people nearby, which helped acclimate them to the Chicago weather they would endure: bitterly cold in winter, blistering hot in summer. It also kept Bloom close to them while he worked on the bigger picture of developing the Midway Plaisance as part of the exposition.

Bloom worked with several exhibitors who had been at Paris and with the contacts developed by World's Columbian Exposition director of publicity and promotions, Moses Handy. Handy was a publicity man a century ahead of his time. He created flyers, broadsides, brochures, and prospectuses that were purportedly sent to every known newspaper and magazine around the world. Additionally, tailored information was sent to specific U.S. cities, fraternal organizations, schools, and corporations—anyone and everyone whom he thought should know about the fair. Handy, as much as any single individual, was responsible for the dynamic array of exhibitors in the Grand Buildings, around the fairgrounds, and on the Midway. Until the final plans for the Midway coalesced, many potential participants were reluctant to locate on what was perceived by some as a secondary location. As Bloom worked his own marketing magic, others began to see the desirability of the Midway blossom.

In virtually all cases, both on the Midway and in the vastly larger and more complex main grounds, location of exhibitors—from the largest to the smallest—was primarily a function of fair management manipulating exhibit spaces like pieces of a very large and elaborate puzzle.

Most countries and many private companies required space in multiple locations: it was common for a large firm or nation to display its products in both Machinery Hall and the giant Manufactures and Liberal Arts Building, for example. And for Germany, Japan, England, or many other countries, it was the norm to be in multiple buildings with sections devoted to individual countries or individual examples of arts and industry. It was also not uncommon for such an exhibitor to have a complete building devoted to its country also serving as a combination museum, reception hall, and temporary consulate.

Each country's needs were unique, and the challenge of accommodating the combined needs of all the countries was onerous. Exhibitors required confirmation of parameters at the earliest possible time in order to facilitate the design, creation, and shipping of materials to Chicago, as well as the printing of brochures, invitations, and trade cards noting each location. Most materials were ultimately printed in Chicago, as many exhibitors were already en route to the city with their exhibits before final confirmation of space or aisle numbers was sent. For example, Krupp Company of Germany, the world leader in munitions and armaments, required its own major building on the grounds, as its massive guns were too large to locate within even the mammoth fair buildings. Like many exhibitors' spaces, Krupp's facility was not completed by the fair's opening. It was a common sight for fairgoers to gaze on nearly completed buildings and partially installed exhibits as they strolled through most parts of the grounds during the early weeks of the fair.

Bloom was responsible for finding and securing exhibitors, but fair management negotiated and executed contracts with the concessionaires. The average fairgoer viewed the German Village, Old Vienna, Chinese Joss House, and other exhibits along the Midway as merely extensions of the appropriate country's exhibits on the main grounds. In part because nationality was promoted dramatically, there was no reason for visitors to consider these exhibits unrelated. In fact, the vast majority of exhibitors on the Midway were private corporations, though in many cases they were funded by their country's government directly or indirectly. The exposition required each Midway concession to be a private entity independent of any other concessions or exhibits on the main grounds and to contract directly with the exposition for Midway space. Exposition management was primarily concerned with the financial arrangements on the Midway. If the Japanese or Turkish governments, among others, were involved with the Midway concessions from those countries, fair management had no concerns as long as the Midway concessions were structured as independent businesses for the purpose of contracting. As such, political and economic issues on the Midway were virtually absent.

The Midway brought together an unprecedented population of human cultures from around the globe. Each concession had a manager who spoke English; many were from the exhibitor's country, but many were hired in the United States.

The Midway operated with none of the social problems one might expect in a community consisting of several dozen disparate groups living and performing together in a miniature city of more than three thousand residents sandwiched into a site just a mile long and six hundred feet wide—not to mention the hundreds of thousands of visitors walking the main street at its center and along the many narrow alleyways of the villages in that unique city. One could easily speculate that creating such a mix of German, Japanese, Austrian, Egyptian, Bedouin, Hungarian, Native American, Scandinavian, Irish, South Sea Islander, American, and other groups

would result in a spate of problems, yet doing so in 1893 along the Midway did not.

There was no "social order" in the placement of Midway exhibitors and their villages. Reviewing the timing of construction and contracts, the placement of exhibitors clearly shows that latecomers received space as and where available. It would have been difficult to determine what locations were more favorable than others. The apparent random placement ultimately met everyone's desires. Smaller concessions were pleased to have the traffic brought in by larger neighbors.

Despite the rapid progress of the new section, Higinbotham and director of works Daniel Burnham still faced the daunting task of finding a centerpiece for the fair, and days and weeks slipped away without any progress. Fair management and its shareholders (who ranged from major Chicago business leaders to thousands of residents who purchased as little as a single share of stock for one dollar) were united in their desire to see Chicago outshine the Paris exposition of 1889. Civic pride was but one of the pressures facing Higinbotham. The Paris exposition was recognized around the globe as the finest and most successful fair of all time. The Eiffel Tower was both the tallest man-made structure on the planet and clearly the most dramatic edifice ever built for a world's fair.

Burnham sent a request to engineers throughout the United States, challenging them to be innovative and to present ideas and plans for a structure that would stimulate interest as dramatically as had the Eiffel Tower, and in the process attract visitors to Chicago from around the world. A major stumbling block among design submissions was the inability of anyone to present an option that could be completed before the fair opened.

Higinbotham and Burnham received an array of enthusiastic designs. The most elaborate were remarkable on paper but generally impractical in reality, unproven in structural integrity, unfeasible financially, and requiring

This attraction, meant to rival the Eiffel Tower, looked rather close to the original. The proposal came with highly detailed drawings, but like virtually all the submissions, it included precious little to suggest that the project could be financed, built in time, or even be structurally possible.

This proposal was for more than a tower structure. The base was a fortlike structure with towers along the perimeter, a sphere rising more than twenty stories, and a cylindrical structure with elevators to take guests to an observation platform at the top. As with all the proposals that preceded the Ferris Wheel, Higinbotham questioned virtually every aspect other than the artistic design.

far more time to complete than was available. One suggestion was a massive globe in which visitors could ride around the earth inside, not totally unlike the Perisphere at the New York World's Fair of 1939–40.

Another looked like a hybrid of a pencil and a missile. Riders would sit in a circle like as-tronauts in the tip of this "rocket" and then be dropped from a substantial height, concluding their trip underground as their vehicle slid into a buried vertical tube.

An intrepid mining engineer suggested an above-ground structure that would provide visitors with information about the process of mining before hurtling them down six hundred feet into the earth in a contraption analogous to a diving bell. After exiting their "ride" they would tour a facsimile of a working underground mine.

Several towers were also proposed, each elaborate in its own way, some with an exhibit or restaurant at the top, bottom, or midpoint. Still another was a massive steel structure that bore a striking resemblance to the Eiffel Tower.

While Frederick Olmsted was successful in turning the Jackson Park quagmire into a Venice of Chicago, and dozens of architects and contractors were equally masterful in creating the ethereal White City, Higinbotham was convinced that he must find something that would make a historical statement and be the signature structure that ensured the fair's success.

As fortuitous as Sol Bloom's arrival was in saving the Midway, the appearance of George Washington Gale Ferris, with drawings in hand, was the providential event that, in the eyes of Higinbotham and Burnham, transformed the fair from good to spectacular. Ferris was an innovative and accomplished bridge-building engineer from Pittsburgh, and unlike the engineers with fanciful proposals who came and were dismissed before him, he had coherent, realistic plans, working drawings, and the reputation and skill to bring his Ferris Wheel to fruition.

Born in 1859, Ferris already had a twelve-year highly successful track record of both designing and building steel bridges, as well as years of inspecting them as a consultant to other engineers and municipalities. His plan was ambitious: a giant wheel that could carry a seemingly impossible 2,160 fairgoers aloft at one time. It featured thirty-six elegant cars the size of streetcars that were attached around what appeared to be a giant bicycle wheel. It would require the largest forged steel axle ever made, not to mention a variety of technical solutions to the complexities of supporting the immense wheel and its components.

Ferris's first trip to Chicago impressed Higinbotham and Burnham, but they still questioned the viability of constructing something

The fifteen-hundred-foot-high Columbus Tower, just one of many proposed structures that were far too elaborate and expensive to be built for the fair, appeared to be vastly more than just a tower. Its first twenty stories appeared to be a castle-in-a-building. Like most proposed structures, this one would contain an elevator to an observation level at the top.

that massive and whether it could withstand the strains of supporting such a load as it revolved.

Ferris left his proposal and drawings with fair management and returned almost immediately armed with testimonials from well-known engineers around the country who endorsed his

The American Underground Mining Exhibit Company's
WORLD'S FAIR MINE
CHICAGO, 1893.
CAPITAL $1.000.000⁰⁰   SHARES $10⁰⁰ EACH.

The World's Fair Underground Mining Company envisioned a project even more difficult than a giant tower—a six-hundred-foot tube carrying visitors to an underground facility where they could observe a working mine.

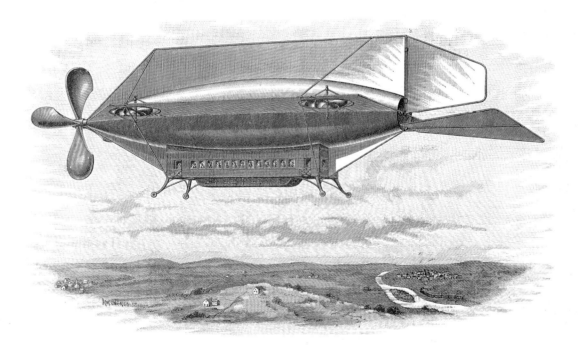

Proposals for a centerpiece attraction to rival the Eiffel Tower included numerous towers, an underground mine, a giant globe, and even an airship. This drawing of the proposed "Carmel Airship" was perhaps a bit ahead of its time. The designer said that his craft was more than seven hundred feet long and could cruise at two hundred mph—not a very realistic speed. Dirigible designs and actual flights had taken place before the Columbian Exposition, but the few successful efforts were overshadowed by the failures—and none were in crafts so ambitiously described as the proposed Carmel Airship, in either size or speed. A decade before the fair, the first ship to fly and return to its point of departure flew a mere five miles in twenty-three minutes.

The Ferris Wheel at the earliest stage of construction probably did not instill confidence that it would be the sound and secure behemoth advertised. The massive pipelike object running horizontally across the image is the steel axle on which the wheel turned, the largest forged steel axle ever manufactured to that point.

design and, most important, its structural stability. He also brought with him commitments for nearly half a million dollars to help finance construction. The latter was almost as important to Higinbotham as the former.

Ferris was given a contract to proceed, but even with his own ambitious schedule endorsed by Higinbotham and Burnham, the world's first Ferris Wheel could not be operational until June, or approximately two months after the six-month exposition opened. Even so, there was virtually unanimous agreement among fair directors that the Ferris Wheel was the centerpiece the World's Columbian Exposition needed. Chicago reporters at the time, clearly

prejudiced in favor of Chicago, commented that the Eiffel Tower was "just" a static structure, "a bridge turned on its end," but the Ferris Wheel was an engineering marvel, as difficult to construct as the great tower and far more impressive in that it revolved!

Nowhere in the fair's official papers was there record of a definitive discussion or details of a decision regarding where to locate the Ferris Wheel. There was undoubtably a feeling that it could not disrupt the design and architectural continuity and elegance of the main grounds, in both appearance and purpose; it was apparently a foregone conclusion that it should be placed in the center of the Midway, which now was

The Ferris Wheel, dominant visually from anywhere on the Midway, towers over the Vienna Café building, which was operated by the concessionaire of Old Vienna. The statue of Pele, the Goddess of Fire, peeks out from behind a tree at the left above the entrance to the Kilauea Volcano.

being referred to as the entertainment center of the fair. After all, what more logical place for the wheel than at midpoint of the mile-long Midway? It does not take a great deal of imagination more than a century later to envision the broad smile on Higinbotham's face as he pictured the giant wheel revolving with more than two thousand passengers gazing awestruck at the Midway below, the buildings of the main grounds, and the view of the sky and Lake Michigan off in the distance.

The virtues of the Ferris Wheel were extolled in the never-ending flow of publicity materials sent out by Moses Handy. Articles throughout the national press were written about the won-drous invention, and as visitors from around the globe planned their visit to Chicago, the Ferris Wheel was at the top their "must see" list.

Higinbotham looked to Bloom and the Midway to generate adequate revenues to ensure profitability for the fair as costs continued to mount with construction nearing completion. The Ferris Wheel was at the center of his financial aspirations. The attractions along the Midway operated a full six months and ultimately did generate the revenue necessary to offset higher-than-anticipated costs, and the Ferris Wheel—despite being operational only four of the six months of the exposition—was a major financial contributor.

The Ferris Wheel was supported by structural steel and a web of wires, besides being sunk in concrete twenty feet below ground to support its mammoth weight. Note the bunting hanging from the lower front of each car—part of the effort to excite the imagination of fairgoers throughout the Midway.

A complete financial breakdown of the revenue generated by all Midway concessions is included in the appendix. As with every world's fair since the first in 1851, no greater measure of success has ever been cited than financial, and without any doubt whatsoever, the Midway was the financial savior of the World's Columbian Exposition.

Every contract on the Midway was negotiated individually by Higinbotham or the financial staff (or both) meeting with representatives from each concession. Standard were terms such as hours one could move freight, hours the exhibit must and could be open, and how revenues were to be recorded and reported to the fair. The only variables were the commission rates to the fair, names of the concession owners, move-in dates, and specific dimensions or structural facts.

There was a brilliance on Higinbotham's part in creating, for the very first time, a separate section of a world's fair strictly for entertainment while the main grounds were devoted to art, history, science, transportation, technology, and educational pursuits in general. In viewing the separation from today's understanding, it was just a beginning. Today we would consider cultural villages not as entertainment but as a major element of the educational segment of a fair. As so often is the case with new ideas, they happen as a response to a situation or a problem. And Higinbotham was faced with the difficult question of finding the best use for the Midway, where to put a growing number of ethnological villages, and the often compelling issue of how to increase revenue.

One American visitor to the fair spent one day of her many at the fair writing a *twenty-page* letter to friends back home, "so I wouldn't forget a thing."

All along the streets near 60th and Stony there were booths where you could invest in popcorn, fruit, lunches, Turkish wares, bird's eye views of the grounds and the *World's Fair Official Guide.*

We found we were in sort of a curiosity shop of all kinds of people, all kinds of houses and all sorts of wares. We came to the conclusion that the greater number were Egyptians and Turks, the latter being especially plentiful in their loose white breeches, scarlet tunics and deep red caps. They have any number of booths where they tempt people with Turkish wares, woods, ivory, jewels and fine embroidery. We saw two particularly beautiful women in these booths dressed in brocaded stuff of the very finest texture.

One of the first things which struck our fancy was the stationary balloon and we stopped to watch them lower and then raise it again.

Next, the DeHomnaite [Dahomey] Village attracted our attention and we stopped to see the natives dancing on the roof.

Then the Chinese Temple, the music here sounded very much as though they were using tin pans but such things have to be cultivated I suppose.

By far the most hideous discord was at the entrance to the Moorish Palace and the people on a close view proved fully as hideous as the music.

We stopped to watch the great Ferras Wheel with its slow majestic movement then onward past the copy of the Leaning Tower of Pisa [clearly misidentified, perhaps the obelisks of the Temple of Luxor] past the Libey Glass Works where they are weaving the dress of glass and silk for the Infantor (the princess or Infante of Spain). [Then] by the Dutch, Irish and Old Vienna and at last under the Illinois Central R.R. bridge and behold before us the White City Proper.

19

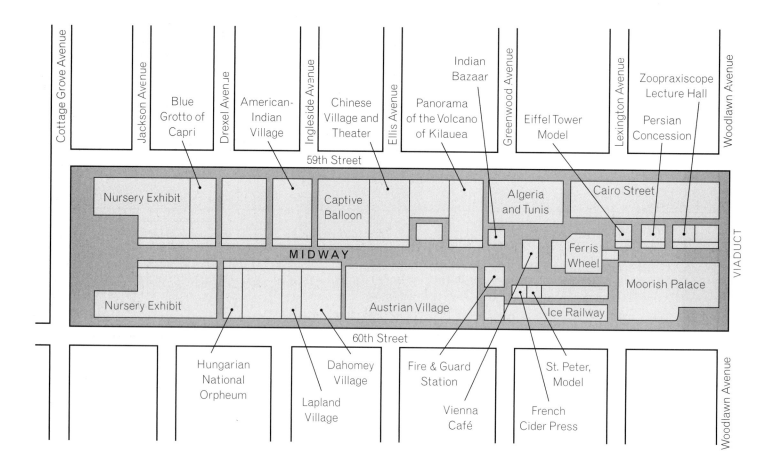

Walking the Plaisance

There were many ways to get to the fair and many possible entrances. One could take a picturesque ride on a Lake Michigan steamer from downtown—pier-to-pier delivery followed by a walk into the eastern edge of the fairgrounds, or even a nickel ride on the Moving Sidewalk. The railroad options for getting to the fair—from across the country or across the city—were as modern and efficient as any in the country, and the various lines all fed into a main entrance on the western edge of the grounds. There were streetcars, taxis, and private carriages—or, for the most ambitious, a healthy six-mile walk from downtown during the spring or fall months. In the virtually unbearable heat of summer, such an option was a near impossibility.

But the most popular entrance to the fair, not just to the Midway, was at the far west, where even in 1893, Cottage Grove Avenue was a very busy north–south thoroughfare clogged with rail traffic, horse-drawn taxis, and private carriages and wagons. The street was perpetually alive with the rumble of wagon and carriage traffic, a hypnotic mixture of hooves and wheels. Every few minutes the rhythmic clickety-clack was broken by the iron-on-iron squeal of a streetcar braking as it eased to a stop between 59th and 60th Streets.

All north–south streets dead-ended into the Midway. Just across 59th Street the new campus of the University of Chicago was welcoming its first students, and large, modern hotels, some still under construction, were changing

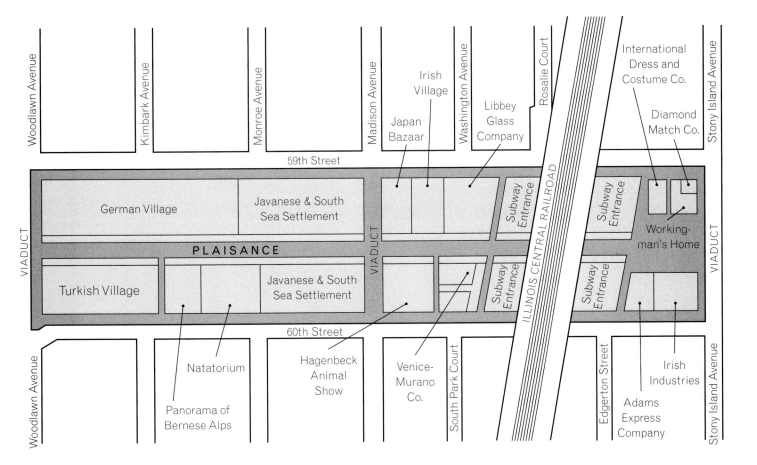

Virtually every Midway map was published before the fair opened, and they all differed in some way from one another, incomplete or inaccurate to varying degrees. The Deere map redrawn here was part of a complimentary handout.

Our walk along the Midway begins at the west end, along the south side. The nursery exhibits at this end were replaced temporarily with a military encampment and also were used for Wild East mock battles. East of that spot, the map shows a nonexistent blank space between the Hungarian National Orpheum and the Lapland Village.

Concession names were often abbreviated or modified on maps. For example, the Austrian Village shown is actually Old Vienna. The enigmatic Camera Obscura was—briefly—nestled among smaller concessions east of Old Vienna.

At the far east end of the south side of the Midway were three small concessions not shown on the map: Submarine Diving, Colonial Log Cabin Restaurant, and Colorado Gold Mine.

Heading back west along the north side of the Midway, the map omits the Electric Scenic Theater, which was located near the Libbey concession. The Aztec Village, created halfway through the fair, was sandwiched in this area as well. Exhibits are not necessarily to scale in relation to the Midway in maps such as this one. The Midway was one mile long and six hundred feet wide, and therefore space often allowed a late concession to be inserted between existing ones.

The oft-misspelled Zoopraxigraphic Lecture Hall was part of the cluster of concessions below Cairo Street, which also included the Panorama of Pompeii, omitted from this map. The American Indian Village was located in the blank spot on the map between the Chinese Village and the Kilauea Volcano but is shown farther west on the map. Finally, not shown at the northwest end of the map were the Brazilian Concert Hall and the very popular Afro-American Ostrich Farm.

Redrawn from *Deere & Company's Indexed Standard Guide Map of the World's Columbian Exposition at Chicago, 1893*. Author's collection.

the neighborhood's landscape in anticipation of the millions of fair visitors who would be arriving.

From Cottage Grove the view to the east was entrancing. Jackson Park had been transformed from a swampland to a wonderland. The massive new buildings of the fairgrounds seemed to float surreally over Lake Michigan; on those all-too-frequent sizzling, cloudless days typical of one of the hottest summers on record in

The crowds poured in like human waterfalls from the western (Cottage Grove) entrance to start the day. One could study a photograph such as this for hours with a magnifying glass, identifying numerous rolling chairs and their attendants, Columbian guards, a man apparently sitting on an awning on the face of Old Vienna (left center), and several dozen white-coated men in the Old Vienna entrance, perhaps restaurant staff or a band gathering to perform.

On a relatively calm and sunny day, an abundance of umbrellas shade men and women from the sun, but the crowd is as sparse as it ever was on the Plaisance. The photo might have been taken toward the end of the day, as most of the foot traffic is heading west, toward the Cottage Grove exit and trains.

Tickets sold at the fair for use on the day of sale (as opposed to the colorful advance ticket, which could be used any time) alternated a letter or letter/number combination to avoid counterfeiting or repeated use. Researchers spent years attempting to uncover the pattern of letter/number combinations. For decades historians and collectors assumed that the numbers used (from 1 to 6 in concert with various letters) represented the months the fair operated. Higinbotham's final voluminous report after the fair closed revealed that the combinations—1/M, 2/F, 3/G, and so on—were totally random. June 1 might have used only the letter "S," while June 2 might have been "6/D" or "2/D".

Chicago, the White City seemed to explode from the blue sky like the pop-up souvenir art books sold on the grounds. "It was if you could reach right out and touch them," Jessie Wilson wrote in her diary.

Pausing at the gate to the Plaisance and squinting into the sun toward the glistening white buildings a mile in the distance, it was easy to become transfixed, mesmerized by the grand sight, until the anxious crowds stepping off the next streetcar began to jostle you in their scramble toward the turnstiles.

Before joining the impatient crowd on the Midway, it was wise to take personal inventory: the ticket in your pocket, a wide-brimmed hat to keep the sun at bay, an umbrella for even more shade in midafternoon, cash and coins, notes, pen, reading spectacles, streetcar schedule, guidebook, and map. The essentials were virtually the same for men and women, all of whom were typically dressed in wool, cotton, or silk, the women in high-collared flowered or solid-colored dresses, the men almost universally in starched collars and ties, dark or beige

suits, and most likely a bowler or straw hat for much-needed shade.

As a breeze blew in off the lake, it would catch the din of untold voices in languages, accents, and pitches virtually all unfamiliar—drifting over and around the eight-foot-high fence to beckon those still outside the gates. There were clean-shaven, handsomely uniformed young men to greet guests with a smile as they approached the gate; they directed each to insert his or her admission ticket in the unique turnstile that would cancel and shred tickets. More than a few visitors grudgingly parted with the beautifully engraved advance-sale admission tickets—with portraits of Abraham Lincoln, George Washington, an American Indian, and, of course, Christopher Columbus. Entrance to the Midway brought a sudden assault on all the senses, including overpowering scents, an engulfing array of pleasing and pungent odors: rich aromas of cooking meats, strong and unusual spices, fresh lemons, a million springtime flowers, *camel or donkey dung*!

Inside the Midway's entrance gate, hundreds of feet ahead but looming so large that men and women had to hold on to their hats as they tilted their heads skyward, the enormous Ferris Wheel rose 264 feet into the air. Few could keep their focus on the exhibits to the left and right as the Ferris Wheel dominated the Midway, drawing them as if in a trance to the massive revolving wheel in the middle of it

23

"We walked a little way around the grounds & came home in time for supper. It was simply a perfect day and the Fair seemed a dream. The boats on the lake seemed to be sailing in the sky."

—Diarist Jessie Wilson after her first visit to the grounds

The guard in the right foreground was no doubt well aware of 1893 photographic requirements and was holding his pose—likely his breath as well—while this picture was taken. An attendant looking very bored sits in his chair outside the entrance to the Dahomey Village.

all. Most fairgoers had read articles about the engineering masterpiece built in record time, but the newspaper accounts hadn't prepared them for the sight of this behemoth the size of a downtown building—and in motion!

It easily took minutes of staring to grasp both its size and its complexity. This "gem of the Midway," as guidebooks called it, had more than fulfilled its designer's promise to rival the Eiffel Tower in engineering prowess and creativity. Suspended from fourteen-story pylons, the enormous wheel and its elaborate webwork of steel carried up to sixty people in each of its thirty-six cabins the size of streetcars. One could only imagine the view from the top before having a chance to ride the Ferris Wheel: how on earth could you describe this colossal contraption in a postcard home so that your recipient could understand and appreciate its grandeur? Fortunately, at least part of that problem could be solved by purchasing photos or books showing not only the great wheel but the Midway surrounding it and the views from it.

The late morning sky was typically cloudless, and the bright yellow-orange sun beat down with a desertlike heat before it was even at its peak in the sky. Visitors, male, female, adult, and child, constantly wiped their foreheads with handkerchiefs and adjusted their hats. Time could stand still once you entered the Midway; facing the mélange of sights, sounds, and smells, one could easily drift into gazing unmoving just a few yards from the entrance gate.

Visitors were more often than not armed with a guidebook—one of many different official world's fair editions from Chicago's Conkey Company or, in lesser numbers, any one of a dozen other privately published editions—studying the description for Concession 58, George Ferris's great wheel, and the other sights along the Midway.

Where to begin was the first dilemma of the day. There were stunning gardens in the nursery exhibits to the right and left, tantalizing aromas tempting the palate, and the sounds of Austrian music just ahead. The only way to begin this globe-circling adventure was to tuck the guidebook back safely under your arm or in your pocket or purse and just start walking.

Most fairgoers, it turned out, selected sights on the Midway that intrigued them most and went straight for them: the German and Austrian Villages one day and late into the evening, the Java Village and the Deep Sea Diving exhibit another afternoon. Interest in specific exhibits and entertainment was, just like at world's fairs today, totally a matter of personal taste.

Logic said to simply start walking, along either the north or the south side of the sixty-foot-wide street in the center of the six-hundred-foot wide Midway; when you finished your day, you could make a mark in your guidebook as to where to start the next day. Fairgoers in 1893 were no different from those today. Some followed the logic of left or right and worked their way through exhibits in careful order. Others sought out the concessions they found most exciting and returned to the same ones repeatedly as their time at the fair allowed. Human nature and preference governed the manner in which millions of visitors chose to enjoy the fair. Compared to today, travel was slow and lifestyles slower. Then, a trip to a world's fair was a once-in-a-lifetime excursion, and families would often spend several weeks at a destination of this magnitude. The pace allowed them to see more than one might today and also to visit favorite sites more times than one could today. Despite large crowds, the expansive grounds were seldom oppressively crowded (except on special days such as Chicago Day, when more than seven hundred thousand attended). And long lines that are commonplace today were not a problem in 1893.

Those relying on their guidebooks could, however, find more confusion than anticipated if they hoped to see the Midway methodically, up one side and down the other in a day or two.

Concessions were all assigned a number by fair management, numerically according to when contracts were signed. And such concession numbers were not exclusive to the Midway. While the Midway was clearly the entertainment center of the fair, there were a variety of revenue-generating concessions scattered about the main grounds. And all restaurants, beverage concessions and kiosks, and sellers of souvenirs, cigars, and other items were assigned numbers as well. Concession 58 was the Ferris Wheel

"I must say, the Fair wouldn't be nearly so pleasant or instructive with the Plaisance left out. As to my morals, they were not injured at all. There are places on the Plaisance but I didn't go to them. I stayed Monday until nearly midnight and mingled with 47 nationalities as they flocked out of their villages to take a little stroll and fill up at the restaurants. It was interesting to see a dozen Javans eating watermelon in a Turkish Café. I had quite a conversation with Toby, who drives the donkey in the Cairo Street, and talked with a number of other people from strange lands. The Plaisance is a great place just before closing time."

—A letter from Frank, a young businessman, to his mother, who was concerned for his safety away from his genteel upstate New York home

Walking the Plaisance

and Concession 3 was the Turkish Village, one of the first to take space on the Midway. But then Concession 9, for example, was the Esquimaux Village (a seemingly logical tenant for the Midway but located instead just off the northeast corner on the main grounds), Concession 36 was the Lowney Chocolate Company (one of several concessions devoted to the sale of confections), and Concession 270 was South Dakota Jewelry in that state's building.

So visitors could draw no inferences as to location by concession number, and in an effort to help, some guidebooks confused the issue even further. Many books printed a schematic of the Midway and assigned their own numbers to exhibitors, simply numbering from left to right on the map.

Larger concessions provided further intended assistance, numbering their own buildings and attractions within the exhibit or village—and since many large concessions included several dozen freestanding buildings or rooms within buildings, large concessions such as Java Village and Cairo Street had numbered "attractions" from one to fifty or more. Consequently, serious study of a guidebook might show three different concessions labeld "Number 40," for example.

Visitors quite quickly learned that the best system for perusing the Midway was simply looking at a map for the name of the attraction and ignoring numbers altogether.

Writing and printing the guides before the fair opened ensured other mistakes. Most every guide, for example, included the Barre Sliding Railway, which was touted as an engineering marvel and entertainment success in Europe, as Concession 1, situated along the southern edge of the Midway. The Sliding Railway was, for whatever reason, a no-show at the fair. Considering the manufacturer's exaggerated claims, it would be easy to speculate that it was an idea that simply never came to fruition. One thing is certain: it never came to the Midway despite reserving space earlier than any other concession, and thus being assigned the number 1. This was the exception rather than rule; still, of 370

concessions awarded, roughly 10 percent never participated in the fair—causing a bit more confusion on both the Midway and the main fairgrounds.

Rides, as we know them today, were sparse in Victorian times. There were electric launches, sailing boats, and gondolas on the waterways of the main grounds, but along the world's first Midway, performance art far overshadowed and outnumbered participatory entertainment. Besides the Ferris Wheel, Ice Railway, and Captive Balloon, the first Midway was starkly different from those that followed over the coming years, decades, and centuries.

Most any time of any day the Midway was crowded with tens of thousands of wandering visitors, walking along the north or south sides, crisscrossing the road from exhibit to exhibit, or walking down the center of the street with a purpose—to reach the main grounds or to trudge toward Cottage Grove after a tiring day of walking miles and seeing but a fraction of what the Columbian Exposition had to offer. The street at the center of the Midway could be nearly elbow to elbow with people, not just visitors but also guards, other fair employees, and various Midway villagers.

Nearly all of the Midway (with the exception of the center street) was allocated to exhibitors, and an amazing volume of entertainment was creatively shoehorned into the space. The only nonexhibitor space was an access road running east and west behind the exhibits on the north side, inside the exterior fence. It was used for wagon traffic servicing the needs of exhibitors, supporting those on both sides of the Midway. There was no such road on the south, where exhibits abutted the exterior fence and railway tracks ran along outside it.

The Cottage Grove Entrance

When entering the Midway from Cottage Grove, visitors were greeted with the mingled scents from the gardenlike nursery on both sides of the street. Some guidebooks mistak-

Carriages at the western edge of the Midway carry the "beauties" from the Congress on Beauty—forty young women performing arts and crafts native to forty different countries. The parade, like many on the Midway, aimed to inspire interest and increase attendance at the concession.

enly listed this open space as practice grounds for military troops at the fair to participate in parades. West Point cadets were housed in tents on the main grounds, but some guides printed prior to the opening listed that space as designated to house troops who would parade at the fair; if in fact it was used for this purpose early on, it was prior to the installation of the nursery. The Wild East's mock battles on camel- and horseback also happened in a portion of this space during later months of the fair.

The first building visitors encountered when entering the Midway was on the right, or south, side just beyond the nursery. The Hungarian National Orpheum and Café was one of the lesser-known facilities on the Midway even though the building's footprint was 75 by 195 feet, relatively large by most nineteenth-century standards. Inside was a theater and concert hall on the main floor, featuring traditional—loud and lively—Hungarian music by one band,

gypsy music by another. There was also a café on the roof garden, and performers and waitstaff were all dressed in colorful billowing traditional garments, as was the norm at all the foreign villages along the Midway.

Local media was drawn to villages offering numerous concurrent events; a concession such as the Hungarian Orpheum that was self-contained in a building with far less flamboyance outside the structure was less likely to attract the attention of reporters—or of fairgoers. And most entering the grounds at the west were pulled as if by a magnet past the first concessions and toward the Ferris Wheel.

Lapland Village

But just east of the Orpheum was a smaller concession, the Lapland Village, that still attracted large audiences. This exhibit, like many, had an entrance charge, but the twenty-five-

The wall surrounding the Lapland Village showed reindeer, hunters, herders, and women at work sewing.

cent fee included various cultural exhibits and entertainment. This village's primary curiosity was the opportunity to see how Laplanders lived and what they wore: colorful and fancy patterned clothing that seemed to belie the rustic appearance of their homes. Performers and hostesses wore brightly decorated costumes, scenes depicting their lifestyle in bright designs on otherwise white outfits, while those tending to herds wore the traditional heavy skin and fur clothing necessary in their native cold climate—and a burden in the Chicago summer.

The Laplanders brought a herd of twenty-six reindeer to the fair, which in itself was an amazing feat and the highlight for many who visited the village. A major event reported by numerous publications and of interest to fair employees, villagers, and visitors on the Midway was the birth during the fair of a baby reindeer, which was named Columbia. Unfortunately, despite all efforts to keep the animals cool and healthy in Chicago, many of the reindeer died during the exposition.

The Lapland and virtually all villages were designed to look exactly as they did in their na-

tive lands, with authentic buildings, dress, food, implements, music, and language—exact replicas of work and daily life. The overwhelming popularity of the Midway was its presentation of genuine exhibits and performances to educate and entertain visitors about populations from around the globe.

Thirty-seven Laplanders lived on the Midway—nineteen men, twelve women, and six children, plus the herd of reindeer and several dogs. Surrounding the village was a very simple eight-foot-high wooden wall painted by several female artisans showing reindeer, hunters, herders, and women at work sewing. Inside, there were no theaters or café, just skin-and-moss homes with rounded tops and a vent for the indoor fire. Still, more than 250,000 fairgoers paid the admission fee to see the village and interact with the reindeer (which virtually none of the visitors had ever seen before) and to talk with the Laplanders and learn about their lives. It's a story repeated dozens of times along the Midway, with the exception of the opportunity to rub noses with reindeer, literally.

In reporting on the fair, several Chicago publications wrote that among the Laplanders were

Here in their village, Laplanders in their fur-and-skin winter clothing are with one of the always endearing reindeer, one of the most popular creatures—human or animal—on the Midway. The Laplanders lived in these traditional huts. They also wore their other traditional garb, brightly colored clothing, for festive occasions and performances. Their beautiful, colorful handmade clothing presented an interesting juxtaposition with their very simple, rustic shelters.

The exterior of the Lapland Village was brightly painted with scenes from their lives—dominated by reindeer running and reindeer pulling a Lap sled. In the foreground is a man with a top hat, holding hands with his children, one of whom is intently watching something on the other side of the street. Children were present at the fair but in relatively very small numbers. Finding one or two in the photos of visitors throughout these pages is not easy.

eight generations of a single family, the eldest of whom was said to be a king of his clan and 112 years old. The story of the generations and the longevity of the "king" originated, not surprisingly, with him! Dozens of publications retold the story as if the king's grandiose claims were factual, without ever questioning the story's credibility.

The rather spry head of the clan said that those accompanying him at the fair included his son (90 years old), grandson (73), great-granddaughter (59), great-great-grandson (41), great-great-great-grandson (29), great-great-great-great-granddaughter (14), and great-great-great-great-great-granddaughter (2). The loquacious king enjoyed remarkable good health for a man of 112, and he seemed to enjoy telling the story of his family almost as much as the local media enjoyed writing about it.

The Lapland Village, with its huts, reindeer, and displays of artwork, clothing, tools, and fishing and hunting implements, was simple. Often dressed in their cold-weather garb, the Laplanders were among the quieter villagers on the Midway. Virtually all those on the Midway were said to be congenial, with an occasional resident described as aloof or curt but seldom rude or irascible. In contrast to the quiet demeanor of the Laplanders, the village just to the east presented a stark difference.

Dahomey Village

The Dahomey Village was populated by one hundred residents of that West African nation, which in 1893 was in the midst of a war with the French (who a year later annexed the country as part of French West Africa). The

The Dahomeyans from western Africa were described to fairgoers as either "intriguing" or "scary." In the center, a rolling chair attendant sits idly waiting for a possible customer. Behind him, the admission ticket office is operated by a pair of young women, probably Chicago-area residents. Concessions often employed locals who were familiar with making change and who could speak English. Just above them, looking anything but ominous, is a Dahomeyan guard. The opposite guard tower is empty, but as long as the temperatures allowed, the Africans had mock guards standing watch to "protect" the village—and to entice potential customers.

French, having spent many years trying to end the slave trade that originated in Dahomey, had expanded their interest to political colonization and control. It was estimated that at one time 20 percent of the Africans taken for the Atlantic slave trade originated in Dahomey. Most Dahomeyans sold into slavery were sold by the Dahomey king, who used the income to purchase, among other things, European weaponry for his army. It was not until 1960 that the country once again became independent; in 1975 it was renamed Benin.

Fairgoers were particularly intrigued by the Africans in part because the roles of the males and females were reversed from what Western-

Journalists reporting on the fair claimed that the Dahomeyans on the Midway were cannibals but that they "restrained their appetites for human flesh while at the exposition."

ers considered normal. Women were warriors and had a reputation for fierceness in combat. The only time they relinquished their military duties was when they were pregnant or nursing.

Along the Midway, the Dahomeyans were seen as the most dramatically "different" from the Americans and Europeans who constituted the vast majority of those attending the exposition. Ironically, it was renowned abolitionist Frederick Douglass who feared that the appearance and performances of these "savages" would reflect negatively on black Americans and reinforce racist attitudes. It is impossible to ascertain what most fairgoers thought, but we can derive an educated opinion based on what many wrote in cards and letters to friends and relatives back home or in their own diaries: the harshest terms they used to describe the Dahomeyans were *scary*, *huge*, and *terrifying*. Still, the Victorian media was mired in derogatory and racist language, freely using terms such as *apes* and *ape-like* in describing the Dahomeyans. (Plate 2 provides a sample of how the media viewed Midway "Character Types.")

The village, managed by a Frenchman (Xavier Pene) who had spent years in the country, consisted of huts segregated by gender. There were small buildings used as a museum and a theater; in the latter, the Africans performed native music, war dances, and other entertainment. The Dahomey Village contained a total of thirty structures.

Hubert Howe Bancroft, a prolific author of studies of ethnic peoples, was a major figure at the World's Columbian Exposition and wrote a multivolume *Book of the Fair*. Bancroft was not college educated, and his parents were prominent abolitionists during the Civil War. One can see his lack of education interspersed in his mountainous writing; when he discussed the Dahomeyans and others on the Midway as part of his exhaustive work on the fair, he wrote as an observer and shared his opinions dogmatically. In 1893 his contemporaries accepted his writing as educated reportage, while today he would be labeled as anything but scientific or academic.

Dahomey Village is at the right, while beyond, the Ferris Wheel dominates the view. In the foreground, under an umbrella, a visitor sits in a wicker-backed "rolling" chair. Wheelchairs were popular at the fair, whether with an attendant or pushed by a family member. With seemingly endless miles of ground to travel in the oppressive Chicago summer heat, it was not the frail or injured who used wheelchairs but the general population, and many thousands of them.

Viewing Bancroft's writing more than a century later, we might label him more uneducated than racist. In reviewing the Africans' musical performance, for example, he noted that "in the centre of the enclosure, if [the theater] can be called that, was the king, a coal-black potentate, sleepy and fat, with thick, bush beard and head and jaws like a bull-dog. His majesty enjoys the music and dancing more perhaps than anything else in life, unless it be the cutting off of heads." The Dahomeyans' theater had open walls with space above them to the ceiling and thatched roof. It was hardly Western in appearance, but it was native to the culture of the Africans.

Bancroft was not impressed with the Africans' music, writing,

> The instruments are as grotesque as the performers, and some of them are fearfully and wonderfully made. The best is a stringed instrument, resembling somewhat the zither. . . . There is an orchestra of drums and bells, with a single flute, a rattle and an ivory horn of most primitive pattern.
>
> The musicians [are] all lean and lank, and all supremely hideous. They wear nose and ear-rings of metal and as little clothing as decency permits, their dark shining bodies showing the scars of many a hard fought battle.

Bancroft sprinkled his opinionated, albeit colorful and detailed, observations with a variety of other opinions with no basis in fact; the idea that the king was a warrior with a history of "cutting off heads" was an example of Bancroft's supercilious "reporting." Bancroft often created odd conundrums in his writing, such as noting that Dahomeyan musical instruments were "fearfully and wonderfully made." There was a strong emphasis on *what* villagers were rather than *who* they were. Bancroft and others felt the need to use a Western filter to describe the appearance of the nonwhite villagers on the Midway. That a music reviewer would consider the size of a musician's nose or a "bulldog" appearance as part of a description of the performance was indicative of the quality of the Victorian media. It also underscores the reason for Douglass's fears that white Americans would be more inclined to compare black Americans to African "savages," endangering the slow progress that black men and women had fought so hard to achieve in the less than three decades since the Civil War.

Since there were regular parades on the Plaisance featuring a variety of villagers from all up and down the street and around the globe, fairgoers often were exposed to the African men and women without having to enter their village. They could also hear the music so painful to Bancroft's ear from the street. But half a million fairgoers paid twenty-five cents each to tour the Dahomey Village after passing by the two guards posted at the exhibit's entrance, placed there in mock protection to reinforce the Africans' fierce demeanor.

Those visitors who stayed past dark mingled freely with a wide array of Midway residents and performers, from Asians to Algerians to Africans, and those who mentioned it in their letters and diaries reveled in those moments. Young women and men alike spoke fondly of the fortuitous opportunities to speak with innumerable Midway residents. Most of those writing correspondence about their experiences were clearly well educated and likewise recognized the rare chance, perhaps the only one they would have, to interact with people whose cultures were so dramatically different from their own.

Visitors consistently spoke of an assault—a positive one—on their senses from Dahomey and all the surrounding villages. The sound of music from myriad sources, a dozen languages filling the air concurrently, and the delicious aroma of cooking from various villages engulfed the Midway from dawn to dark. When the wind whipped across the main fairgrounds off Lake Michigan, it hardly slowed as it swept down the Plaisance, making it all but impossible to identify the individual components of that sensory onslaught. The only problem for fairgoers who sought to pursue the source of the tantalizing smells and compelling sounds was to determine where they originated.

Old Vienna

Next to the generally loud and, to some, menacing Dahomeyans was Old Vienna, which stretched well over a city block from east to west, on a plot of land that was over one hundred thousand square feet. Old Vienna was a walled city with homes, stores, and restaurants, built as a facsimile of the city as it was during the seventeenth and eighteenth centuries.

The exterior city walls were covered with a faux stone finish similar to the plaster, cement, and hemp "staff" that coated all the exteriors of the whitewashed main buildings on the fairgrounds. Around Old Vienna, the walls were not stark white but created to look spotty and flawed, as if they had been built hundreds of years earlier. Old Vienna was a facsimile of the earlier city in its outward appearance, including the castlelike turrets and steep roofs on two-story buildings.

Admission of a quarter opened the world of Austria on many levels. The village included an enormous staff of five hundred Austrian men and women, the majority involved in food service. Visitors entered through massive gates flanked by large towers. The interior storefronts and houses were arranged in a circular fashion facing a main courtyard. Large structures inside the city included a theater where two different Austrian bands performed daily at no additional charge, a church (in use throughout the fair), and a beer garden. Old Vienna was patterned after the city's Graben district, dating to Roman times, which today is the main, bustling shopping area of central Vienna. Included with admission to the city was entrance

Old Vienna, designed to look as the city did in the eighteenth century, had a worn and bedraggled appearance by design, which seemed part of its charm and certainly did not deter any fairgoers from visiting.

Old Vienna is quiet in this morning view before the fair opened. Shown is the courtyard cafe. The cordoned-off area of rows of chairs to the left was for a band performance, while the tables and chairs to the right were for beverage and food service. Note that the wooden chairs in rows were a sturdier hardback chair, while those at the right (also wooden) were folding chairs.

Many of the Midway exhibits and concessions exhibited sophisticated marketing for the Victorian era. Cairo Street and its historical museums and contemporary city streets circulated a variety of handbills and sold various programs within the exhibits.

the clock in farmhouses and various structures inside the city.

Noted in catalogs as "Booth 50" in Old Vienna—underscoring the confusing various methods of numbering concessions, structures, and villages—was part of a phenomenon within the fair as a whole. The World's Columbian Exposition spawned a mini numismatic industry of its own, producing, by most estimates, more than five hundred different medals to commemorate the fair and Columbus's voyage. An important group of these were for sale in Old Vienna. Overall they ranged from small, relatively pedestrian souvenir tokens without much artistry to some of the world's foremost medallic artwork. A medal generally regarded today as one of the most beautiful to have come from the fair was struck in both bronze and white metal in Milan by Stefano Johnson and designed by an artist known at the fair simply as Professor Pagliaghi. Versions were struck from separate dies in English and Italian and in multiple sizes. The obverse featured a bust of a balding Columbus with curly hair cascading over his ears, and around the perimeter were a Native American and what was assumed to be a European reaching out to one another below a globe. The reverse was an artistic scene of a person with angelic features "floating" above an individual on the ground, while around the perimeter in small type were the names of all the states in the United States as of 1893. Because dozens of medals featured a portrait of Columbus and dozens more featured a scene of Columbus's landing in the Americas, many medals have become known over the years either by their designer's name or some other unique moniker. The Johnson/Pagliaghi medal, for example, is known simply as the Stefano Johnson medal. Others have odd nomenclature such as the Ruffled Collar Columbus or Navigator Columbus (because he is pictured holding a nautical map).

It is almost impossible to identify many of the specific sellers, concessions (or those working under the auspices of someone else without

to a museum the Austrians claimed was the finest on the Midway. It may well have been. It included early European paintings and artifacts from ancient Rome and Egypt (including a mummy). As with a surprising number of Midway village exhibits, many of the offerings were not limited to the native village, city, or exhibit. Old Vienna was perhaps the most eclectic of all on the Plaisance, gathering art and artifacts from throughout the world. Nearly half of the staff of Old Vienna lived there around his or her own concession), and locations where the many styles of medals were sold. Many were available in Chicago stores and advertised for sale in the daily programs of the fair as well as in magazines and Chicago newspapers. The Stefano Johnson medals were available in only two fair locations—at Booth 50 in Old Vienna and at the La Rabida Convent (a replica of where Columbus once stayed) at the far east edge of the main grounds.

Old Vienna contained forty-nine other separate stores and houses, the largest being the main town hall and restaurant. The latter could seat up to one thousand diners in its casual open outdoor courtyard (plate 3), where a chance of inclement weather was unlikely in the smoldering Chicago summer. Its custom-made chairs—manufactured in Chicago—were an unusual type of folding wooden chair. Rather than folding up with the seat facing the back, as with most such chairs, they opened into a "Z" design with a separate piece of slatted wood extending below the seat for extra support. The dining hall, which served a complete Austrian menu, was one of two large restaurants operated by Old Vienna; the other was the Vienna Café, outside the walled city just to the east, next to the Ferris Wheel in the center of the Midway.

A variety of merchants filled the shops in Old Vienna—and many, like Booth 50, had absolutely nothing to do with their host, nor were many Austrian. Old Vienna provided the space for artisans and manufacturers to sell their goods in an 1893 version of a mall.

Several of the storefronts inside Old Vienna sold world's fair souvenirs, Viennese crafts, artwork, jewelry, and more. But Booth 50 offered a special glycerine toothpaste; "the pencil that never needs sharpening" (a series of small leads nesting in one another that could be replaced when the one below was dull); the Johnson/Pagliaghi Columbus medals; a cane hollowed out to hold both a half pint of the owner's favorite beverage and a single glass; "Moldawidt" diamonds (probably the green tektite/meteorite "gems" sold today as moldavite from the Czech Republic) that were advertised as the finest diamond substitutes available in the world; and mother-of-pearl and ivory items. And for those wanting to avoid a trip to one of the medical stations on the grounds, Old Vienna even had one entrepreneur selling the Pocket-Dispensary, a case containing eighteen different remedies and articles, "to be employed with certain success as first help in indisposition, wounds and various accidents." Throughout the publications and guides circulated at the fair, Old Vienna was touted for its authentic Austrian cuisine and equally authentic Austrian military bands—and the largest bazaar of shops anywhere on the Midway. Since these entrepreneurial sellers were generally not licensed by the fair with their own concessions, their revenue was reported in a lump sum along with Old Vienna's. In the unusual case where a seller had a fair concession to sell an item or items and did so within another concession, it was up to the larger concession and the entrepreneur to arrive at contractual terms between them, with the gross sales always being reported by the licensed concessionaire only.

At the Center of the Midway

Just beyond Old Vienna, the Midway continued along the road to the east and also branched out into a cluster of structures in the center of the Plaisance, forming a bustling hub of activity surrounding the Ferris Wheel. On the north side was Bloom's Algerian and Tunisian Village, followed by the most popular site on the Midway, Cairo Street.

Just east of Old Vienna was the start of the Ice Railway, and next to it, the Moorish Palace. In the center of this day-and-night excitement, between Woodlawn and Greenwood Avenues, stood what was praised—and advertised—as the mechanical wonder of the fair, and often of the age, George Ferris's big wheel.

The small group of buildings abutting Old Vienna included a fire and guard station, generally of minimal use during the fair. Occasion-

The Algerian and Tunisian Village was managed by Sol Bloom, who was also responsible for the management of the entire Plaisance. Stands such as the one at right were seemingly everywhere and were not listed on maps as were the villages and larger concessions. It's not possible to see what this kiosk was selling, but it was likely either souvenirs from the Algerian and Tunisian Village or some type of beverage—water, cider, soda—which outsold every other item available at the fair.

The Algerian Theater, managed by Sol Bloom, was one of the few international theaters that came to Chicago after having performed four years earlier at the 1889 Paris exposition.

Riders on the Ferris Wheel had an expansive and captivating view to the east. The entire eastern portion of the Midway unfolds from below the giant wheel. Cairo Street is at the immediate left, the bright blue dome of the Moorish Palace to the right. The puzzlelike interlocking of the various concessions, including substantial original greenery on the north side of the Midway, illustrates how planners were able to create the feeling of villages seemingly miles away from the outside world. Beyond the Plaisance are the various domed roofs of the main grounds: left to right, the low domes of the Art Palace and Horticulture Building, the tall and narrow dome of the Illinois Building, the U.S. Government Building, the enormous Manufactures and Liberal Arts Building, and at the far right, the Administration Building.

ally the Columbian guards dealt with someone climbing the wall to gain entrance, the easiest access being the wall adjacent to the freight road behind the Midway buildings. The guards walked a beat here as on the main grounds, helping with heat stroke as often as with crime. Considering the hundreds of storefronts and booths throughout the Midway, the Plaisance was surprisingly crime free.

There were also several small concessions tucked behind the guard station and the southeast corner of Old Vienna.

The French Cider Press was a favorite stop for the unique experience of watching an authentic Normandy apple press squeeze Jonathans and Spies into juice for two cents a glass. Perhaps even more popular were the *cidre doux* (alcohol content 2.5 percent) and, for the hardier drinkers, the *cidre brut* (alcohol content 4 percent), sparkling fermentations of apple juice.

Next to the French cider was the *least* popular of all Midway attractions, gauging by financial

measure: the elaborate scale model of St. Peter's Basilica in Rome. The model was created not for the fair but between the sixteenth and eighteenth centuries. Constructed from original drawings by Michelangelo, it measured approximately 30 feet in length, 15 feet in width, and 15 feet in height, an exact scale model of the actual church and its facilities in Rome. The exterior of the structure was stucco and faux marble, and inside were faithfully reproduced frescoes and artwork to scale. In the same exhibit building were several other scale models, including the Cathedral of Milan (carved in wood), the papal Piambino Palace (wood), St. Ahnese Church (marble), and the Roman Pantheon of Agrippa (wood). The models were unique, certainly worthy of attention from anyone who admired delicate scale models and antiquities, yet fewer than twenty-five thousand visitors chose to spend the twenty-five-cent admission fee to view the miniature churches during the six months of the fair. Instead, visitors seemed to favor sam-

This photo of the Papal Saint Peter's exhibit was taken perhaps on its dedication day, but most certainly prior to the fair's opening. To the left, a structure is barely under construction, but literally hundreds of thousands of visitors wandered the main grounds and the Midway in the six months or more before the fair opened. Perhaps the formality of this exhibit contributed to its abject failure. It may have seemed more daunting than inviting to have half a dozen guards looking like brightly painted toy soldiers "guarding" the entrance. Only about four thousand visitors per month viewed the ancient scale models displayed here.

listed on at least one fair map and described in some guidebooks, but since most were printed before the opening of the fair, a few inaccuracies were inevitable. Taking any of the guides as gospel was ill advised for fairgoers and has been equally as problematic for historians.

When a fair visitor's estate was sold late in the 1990s, it included a small number of souvenirs from the World's Columbian Exposition—including the only known Camera Obscura ticket. Although at least one fairgoer had a ticket, the fair apparently never consummated a contract with the company (since no concession number was ever assigned). Thus, Camera Obscura remains an enigma until some researcher happens upon an explanation. It is possible that the attraction was being built while negotiations for a concession license were in progress and that the ticket was sold or given to one of the tens of thousands of visitors touring the grounds before the official opening of the fair.

During construction, visitors, for a quarter, were given full access to wander both the main grounds and the Midway. One assumes that many areas were cordoned off as work was under way, but apparently the main buildings of the White City presented an interesting enough sight to tantalize visitors and leave them anxious to return when the fair opened. Bloom, in discussing his Algerian concession and his purview over the entire Plaisance, said that an ample number of visitors wandered through the partially constructed Midway and spent both time and money at many concessions. In fact, he claimed that by the time the fair opened, his Algerian village had already broken even

pling the breadth of offerings in most villages, where they could easily spend an entire day or more, or standing in line for the magnificent Ferris Wheel. Also knowing that they could see a million artifacts on the main grounds with no admission charge, it is not difficult to see why a scale model of St. Peter's Cathedral might be low on the priority list. Considering the vast array of sights one could enjoy on the Midway for the same quarter—in rough terms more than $6.00 in today's dollars (using the approximate multiplier of 25)—the beautiful miniature of St. Peter's was presumably passed over by all but those with the most disposable income.

Next door—at least briefly—to the sparsely visited model of St. Peter's was what one might consider the best-kept secret on the Midway: Camera Obscura, Trees of Wonder. This concession—given no number in the fair's financial records—*may* have been open for business for a short time, but it is difficult to confirm. It was financially. That might be an exaggeration, but it's clear that many Midway concessions, even if not prepared to show all their wares, were happy to collect their own admission fee for a glimpse of their incomplete village or exhibit.

Given Bloom's description of pre-opening business along the Midway, it is quite plausible that the Camera Obscura was in a similar pre-opening phase while its concession contract had not been finalized. By the time opening day arrived, it was probably unfinished, possibly out of funds, and most likely closed before the fair gates ever opened.

One catalog, probably citing promotional text from the would-be concessionaire, said that the Camera Obscura exhibit was something exciting that most fairgoers had never experienced and should not miss. The concept of the camera obscura is to focus a narrow beam of light into a box—which could be handheld or up to room-sized, as it no doubt would have been if built on the Midway—and reflecting it outward to display an image on some type of screen. Leonardo da Vinci, among many scientists over the years, experimented with and explained the principles, which theoretically could be considered a precursor to the camera. Regardless of interest in the display planned for the Plaisance, it failed to leave the starting gate.

Ice Railway

Just behind the space at least preliminarily allocated to the Camera Obscura, parallel to the

This is a view of the Ferris Wheel from just off the Midway. The white covered track in the foreground at the right is the Ice Railway, where toboggan-like vehicles strung together took visitors twice around the enclosed snow- and ice-covered track. The large chimney is from the power plant manufacturing the artificial ice for the track.

exterior wall of the Midway, was the one attraction that might be identified as a "ride" such as one would expect on later midways.

The Ice Railway was an enclosed track with an artificial ice slope akin to a roller coaster: riders were towed slowly up a slope and then released to race down a hill and continue along a level surface until they stopped. A mechanized pulley took the riders up to the top of the twenty-five-foot hill and then released them for a free-fall down the slope and around the 850-foot track. Each of the coaster "trains" consisted of four toboggan-like vehicles attached to one another carrying up to sixteen riders per toboggan; the toboggans operating on the 44.5-inch wide track were fitted with rubber side bumper wheels so that the train maintained a straight, smooth ride. The building at the west end, where riders began and ended the journey, also included a restaurant.

The De La Vergne Refrigeration Machine Company employed thirty workers at the concession and provided the power plant and icemaking machinery to keep the ride smooth and cool. Early guides to the fair wrote that an ice skating rink was to be situated at the beginning of the Ice Railway. The rink would have been indoors, necessarily so due to the summer heat, and a welcome respite for any of the summer guests inclined to escape the weather and enjoy themselves. Ice Railway advertising called it "the sleighing . . . [that] will make you cool, comfortable and happy." The cost for two trips around the ice track was a dime, a bargain compared to other attractions. Nearly seven hundred thousand people availed themselves of the unequivocally coolest spot on the Midway. Unfortunately, as a result of the railway's enclosure under its domelike roof, there are no known photographs of passengers sleighing on the Midway.

As early as 1890, De La Vergne, based in New York city, had become a world leader in the manufacture of refrigeration machines; producing artificial ice for the Ice Railway was an easy process given its prowess with the machinery.

The company reportedly grossed about $2 million annually around the time of the fair, equivalent to roughly $50 million in today's economy.

De La Vergne's equipment was used in ice plants, breweries, and cold storage facilities, among others. The company's successes continued with the Ice Railway and positive publicity in Chicago and national newspapers. The *Chicago Herald* said the obvious during the fair, that "it seems incredible that World's Fair visitors in July can take a sleigh ride on real snow. The Ice Railway is one of the leading attractions on The Midway Plaisance." De La Vergne exhibited its machinery at the fair in the Government, Agricultural, and Machinery halls and credited the ride's popularity as instrumental in bringing traffic to its three exhibits on the main grounds.

A report said that a crash of the Ice Railway killed a rider and injured others, but it was never confirmed by exposition management and was not mentioned in the Columbian guard's report on crime, injury, and death.

Adjacent to the Ice Railway, in the center of the Midway, was the extension of Old Vienna, the Vienna Café—one of the most popular restaurants on the Plaisance. Besides the café, the building housed a large theater, a dining hall, and several smaller eating areas.

The Ferris Wheel

Directly behind the Ice Railway was the mammoth Ferris Wheel (plate 4), the fair's landmark attraction, towering 264 feet over the Midway. Little else of the Midway could be seen across the mile or two from where fairgoers might be standing in the White City, unless they had taken that relatively new invention, the elevator, to the top of the Manufactures and Liberal Arts Building.

Riding the giant wheel was like taking a leap into the future. The colossal wheel staggered the imagination on many fronts: It was larger than any nonbuilding structure most fairgoers had ever seen. It was taller than any building in the United States other than a small handful in New York or Chicago. At 264 feet the Ferris Wheel was a scant 38 feet shorter than the Masonic Building, Chicago's first "skyscraper," which had opened the year before the fair.

But at a time when craning one's neck skyward was reserved for following a flock of birds or gazing at interesting cloud formations, there was much more to the Ferris Wheel than its height. Sitting or standing in a car hanging on an 825-foot-circumference wheel was so far beyond everyone's experiences that most simply gazed quietly; the rare exception was the passenger overcome with vertigo or fear who punctuated the incredibly quiet ride with a momentary scream.

The cars emulated a posh version of a street- or railcar, each measuring 27 feet long and 13 feet wide with a comfortable and surprising 9-foot-high rooftop. Claustrophobia was never a problem. Each car could accommodate a maximum of sixty riders and was fitted with rotating metal chairs attached to the floor. Unlike in modern amusements, riders were free to stand, and the majority freely wandered gazing out the windows in each direction. The Ferris Wheel staff consisted of a conductor for each car who acted as tour guide, doorman, and security agent in case someone should act compulsively or dangerously (which reportedly never happened). There was also a small staff of ticket takers, mechanics, and management personnel. The wheel rotated west to east, with passengers facing toward the fairgrounds and Lake Michigan as they rode.

The vast majority of the riders had little interest in the properties and construction of the wheel, as long as they were assured of its safety. Daniel Burnham, George Ferris, and Moses Handy, of course, were publicly proud of the engineering triumph that made possible the spectacular fifty-cent, twenty-minute journey (for two revolutions). The wheel hung like a giant's bicycle wheel on an axle resting on the two towers. The supports were sunk in twenty feet of concrete below the surface, and the axle—the largest forged in the world at the time—was 45.5

feet long and 33 inches in diameter and weighed nearly 90,000 pounds. The wheel was enveloped by a structure that included wide stairways to staggered platforms at multiple elevations, allowing several cars to be loaded and unloaded simultaneously. There were also offices for staff responsible for safety, maintenance, and financial records.

While most riders wanted time on the Ferris Wheel in the middle of the day when the sky was clear and visibility the best, there were always crowds late in the evening, as well. The wheel was lit up after dark with three thousand incandescent bulbs; the fair as a whole was illuminated by more electric lights than existed in homes and businesses in the entire city of Chicago in 1893. Nighttime was special on the main grounds, where fireworks often exploded above the lagoons, and along the Midway, where oil lamps and electric lights were interspersed, illuminating the mile-long carnival atmosphere.

The wheel was the perfect Victorian combination of inventive construction, elegant interior, and awestruck passengers. It met all of fair management's and engineer-inventor Ferris's goals for fairgoer interest and excitement and engineering success. But for George Washington Gale Ferris, this success fell short of expectations. Ferris's interpretation of his contract and management's view of the same left a gap between the two parties of more than $84,000 (more than $2.1 million in today's dollars) when the fair closed. After operating only four of the fair's six months, the Ferris Wheel generated gross revenue of more than $733,000 and hosted 366,500 riders. But a protracted lawsuit dragged on between the fair and Ferris long after the Midway began to revert to its earlier state as a quiet boulevard. When the inventive Ferris died a few years later at just thirty-seven years of age, the legal conflict was still unresolved.

Ferris's legacy did not just live on but grew virtually overnight as wheels of all sizes began to dot countrysides across the United States and around the world. The Ferris Wheel was the bon vivant of the fair—and history—but that first and most ingenious and elegant wheel was destined for an ignominious end.

That first wheel operated for a few days after the fair officially closed to accommodate visitors who had to have that one more ride or had somehow managed to miss their chance while the fair was still open. Afterward it was moved briefly to a location in Chicago on Clark Street where it intersected with Lincoln Park. A ride on the world's first Ferris Wheel and a vaudeville performance before or after cost just a quarter. A group of local businessmen envisioned building an amusement park—a *midway*—with the wheel at its center, but the plan was a robust failure.

The wheel sat idle for nearly a decade before being disassembled and moved to St. Louis for the 1904 Louisiana Purchase Exposition. It was reported to be a good revenue generator of gross revenue, but unfortunately not sufficiently to show a profit. Regardless, the ridership and revenue in St. Louis were a fraction of that at the World's Columbian Exposition, perhaps because in that one intervening decade, Ferris wheels (albeit simpler and smaller) had become commonplace at parks and fairs around the world. Also, the opportunity to gaze out over the landscape from 264 feet above the ground simply was no longer the novelty it had been. Perhaps it was best that its inventor had passed away, as after the St. Louis fair closed, furniture, parts, and fittings of the once glorious and unparalleled wheel were removed and sold, and the skeletal remains were dynamited into a heap of metal sold to scrappers.

Moorish Palace

Underneath and to the south of the breathtaking ride of the Ferris Wheel was the most colorful structure, the Moorish Palace, domed in a reflective blue. The fair's main grounds, the White City, were stark by design to present a marble or alabaster appearance. The Midway, by contrast, was a product of the diversity of its exhibits and villages. Virtually all the visual

record of the Midway comes from publication sketch artists and the burgeoning business of photography. The understanding of the colorful people, shops, and villages exists either in text or in paintings of them. Tens of thousands of images exist of performers, guards, fairgoers, and men and women with different shades of nonwhite skin. Because of the limitations of the media, visitors appear dressed in black-and-white suits and black-and-white solid or patterned dresses.

The Moorish Palace management had no difficulty with modesty or a lack of it. The brochure noted that the concession contained "startling wonders . . . the chief attraction of (The) Midway Plaisance." The poem on the cover tells little about what was inside the great palace, although it at least alluded to the oddities of mirrors, maze, and excessive gilding.

This photo was taken from the Ferris Wheel looking east, but unlike many others, it was taken when the Ferris Wheel car was somewhat close to the ground as opposed to being at the apex of the revolution. The result was that little of the main grounds was visible, with the exception of the tall, thin dome of the Illinois Building near the left side of the photo.

Fortunately, several artists painted Exposition scenes, and none was busier on the Midway than Charles Graham, who left us with colorful realities of reds, blues, greens, and yellows along the Midway, the major subject of scores of his watercolors. His paintings complemented the stories and reports of myriad visitors who had no idea how invaluable to the history of the Midway their brief descriptions to parents, siblings, and friends would be, from "the blinding reflection off the blue dome" of the Moorish Palace to "the beautiful green and red brocaid [*sic*] of the Asian dancers" to "the deep blue waters of the grotto of Capri."

The huge Moorish Palace dome was omnipresent in photos of the Midway even as it was dwarfed by the Ferris Wheel. It could reflect the bright sun into the cars of the Ferris Wheel, ensuring that every rider was aware of it even

if they had been idly staring straight ahead. Depending on the time of day and where a fairgoer might be walking along the Plaisance, the overpowering summer sun created prismatic reflections off the blue dome. Ads for the Moorish Palace in local papers and guides advised fairgoers simply to look for "the large blue dome" on the Midway.

The Midway was indeed as colorful visually as it was to all the other senses. When viewing the mile-long Plaisance as recorded on Graham's canvases, as opposed to the myriad photographs of the street, it is as if someone switched on a light to reveal the colorful uniqueness of every village and villager.

Broadsides posted on and off the grounds emphasized to all that the Moorish Palace was "a place where you can take ladies and children." In fact, despite infrequent concerns voiced by

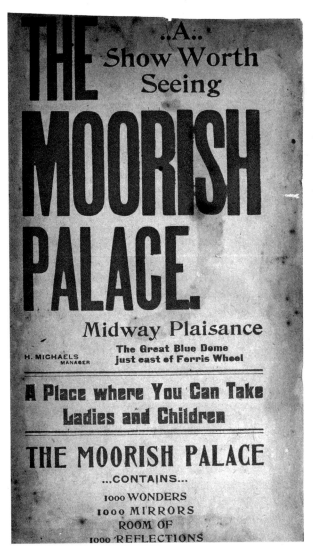

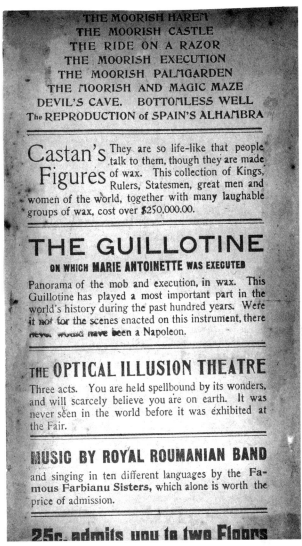

This handbill *[two halves, cut vertically, so 15 inches long]* is from the Moorish Palace, which more than anywhere other than perhaps Old Vienna featured a collection of international exhibits and oddities.

the more conservative elements of Victorian society, the entire Midway was a place where one could take women and children without fear for their moral well-being.

Upon entering the dome, visitors were awed by another dramatic show of light and reflection—a labyrinth of mirrors that could capture both the viewer's imagination and his or her image by the score. The complex maze of mirrors often resulted in visitors needing the assistance of a guide to help them to move on. Once free, they could enjoy a wide variety of exhibits, art, music, shopping, food, and more within the domed structure.

The mazelike interior of the first floor was resplendent in what was advertised as "authentic Moorish art and architecture," rows of gilded and painted columns leading from the mirrored pathway into the heart of the building. The archways and pillars continued in labyrinth fashion, but there were no optical illusions to disorient the visitors; pillars were not much taller than a person, but they supported massive archways to ceilings fifteen feet high.

The floors were made of mosaic tiles, and while the interior and exterior were both inspired by Moorish structures from the previous several hundred years, the building was designed by Chicago architect August Fiedler.

Like at many of the concessions, the operators stressed the realism of the native culture presented. Still, like Old Vienna, with its odd collection of vendors in the bazaar, many concessions offered what could only be described as a peculiar blend of entertainment and souvenirs.

The Moorish Palace contained a serene Palm Garden, "a scene of true Oriental beauty [where] we can imagine ourselves on the north coast of Africa," according to that same advertising poster.

The primary musical entertainment in the Moorish Palace was provided by the Roumanian [sic] Royal Concert Band, led by J. Negreskou, violinist and solo tenor. The band, consisting of twelve male and four female musicians, played daily beyond the labyrinth and through the corridors. The Farbianu Sisters performed with the band, singing songs said to be presented in ten different languages during the performances. The Moorish village also, unexpectedly, featured a Scottish Highland dancer, a popular clown named "Sparrow," and an entourage of more than sixty historical wax figures, including Abraham Lincoln.

Despite the very un-Moorish origins of much of the collection in the palace, the wax figures, dioramas, and museums were extremely popular. The wax museum was part of an emphasis on death on the second floor, as it wasn't just Lincoln on display, but rather a diorama of his assassination in lifelike wax. In a bloodbath in wax that might have shocked women, children, *and* men, another scene featured "a ride on the razor." Here, one who had incurred a sultan's wrath was slid down a thin-edged razor from "a tremendous height to a bottomless pit." The pit was not so bottomless, however: fairgoers could peer into it to see the victim, "one half on either side . . . in the pool of blood below."

There were also such scenes as "A Moorish Execution," "Public Punishment in the Middle Ages," "The Dying Zouave," and, on the lighter side for the whole family, "Sleeping Beauty" and "Little Red Riding Hood."

Just beyond the chamber of wax horrors was an entire gallery devoted to the execution of Marie Antoinette, which included what were "certified" as the genuine scaffold and guillotine used in her execution. Around the centennial of her execution, visitors could "enjoy" her beheading in lifelike wax. If these bits of entertainment were not sufficient, there was yet more for the eye and mind—an optical illusion theater where a statue alternated between dripping realistic blood from marble and turning into a live woman, and then back again to a bleeding statue.

Like other large concessions, the Moorish Palace also had a restaurant and did a brisk business in light snacks, lunches, and beverages. The palace charged twenty-five cents for entrance to its museum (including the wax figures and various artifacts and examples of historical weaponry) and theater, while some of its smaller attractions required a ten-cent ticket. The Mosque of Tangiers, was, like most attractions, a replica of what would be found in the homeland, and here it also was used as a house of worship for the many Muslims who worked and populated various Midway concessions. There was no question about the authenticity of the villagers, their attire, and the myriad performances and culinary delights they offered. Besides the demonstration of national pride in exhibits, performances, and clothing (as was the norm in virtually all concessions on the Midway), there was another important goal: profitability. Merchandise unrelated to the nationality of the village was commonplace as long as it generated revenue.

But within the Moorish Palace, as with every "ethnic" village, display, restaurant, or concession, the commitment to authenticity was paramount and advertised unceasingly. Each village presenting a glimpse of life from around the globe offered accurately reproduced structures, entertainment, and perspective regarding another culture's lifestyle.

Turkish, Bedouin, and Persian Villages

Just east of the domed Moorish Palace was the eighty-five-thousand-square foot Turkish Village, which like its fellow exhibitors combined a variety of cultures and entertainment in one very large enclosure. There was no charge to enter the village, but many of the features inside required an admission fee. The Turkish Theater or "Oriental Odeon" was the concession's marquee entertainment; admission was fifty cents, the same as a ride on the Ferris Wheel or admission to the fair itself. (For an additional ten cents you could purchase a souvenir program [plate 6].) The feature was a three-act play, *Antar the Son of Sheddad*, performed by a cast of sixty-five male and female actors assembled from Jerusalem, Bethlehem, Nazareth, Damascus, Aleppo, and Constantinople. The play was accompanied by a full orchestra. The

In the Turkish Village, Elia Souhami Sadullah of Constantinople sells a variety of goods typical of Midway vendors—tables, ceramics, Oriental rugs, pipes, and more. Far Away Moses (third from left with the white beard), a ubiquitous figure on the Midway, seemed to be in photos most everywhere. He was said to have been a guide for Mark Twain when the writer visited the Middle East.

Turkish sedan chair carriers rest while there is a lull in the demand for their services.

The Persian Palace featured entertainment, exhibits, and souvenirs similar to other Middle Eastern villages. Hubert Bancroft singled out this concession, however, for offering dancers of "questionable character." They were, by other reports and photographs, no different in their attire or performances from those on Cairo Street, at the Turkish Village, or at the Algerian theater, but perhaps on the day Bancroft visited Persia, there was a little more undulating in the dances than normal.

A group of Turkish performers shows off the various blades they used to tantalize the audience with their dexterity and danger in performances and mock battles. The always popular—especially with journalists—Far Away Moses is in the second row center with the white beard and fur garment draped around his neck.

freestanding theater building featured a large lobby and theater seating for fifteen hundred; elaborate twin towers flanked the entrance.

Separate entertainment under the aegis of the Turkish Village included a Bedouin Encampment (twenty-five-cent admission) and a Persian Tent (also twenty-five cents). The highlight of the Persian Tent exhibit, according to the concession's literature and local newspaper reports, was a massive solid silver bed (said to weigh three thousand pounds) that had been the property of a sultan. While a broad array of foods and souvenirs were available, not surprisingly in great demand were Turkish coffee and cigarettes.

One of the many unique offerings on the Midway was a sedan chair available in the Turkish Village. Two men carried the "chair" and the guest—for a fee of seventy-five cents per hour—either on a brief journey through the village or to a destination of his or her choice on the Midway. The sedan chair was a simple apparatus, a small booth (similar in appearance to a wooden telephone booth) in which the rider could sit, with poles approximately twelve feet long fitted through metal brackets on each side. The sturdy poles tapered to about two inches in diameter at each end so the attendants could grip them. They hooked the poles through cloth bands worn over their shoulders, holding the poles in each hand near the ends; then it was off on a leisurely ride along the Midway like a visitor in nineteenth-century Constantinople. A Chicago reporter noted that "their tops protect their occupants from the sun, and the slight motion produced by the steady trot of the bearers is much pleasanter, when one becomes accustomed to it, than the jostling of the or-

This Turkish clown played the role of foil in various performances in the Turkish Theater, akin to the early Keystone Cops of silent movies, alway there to take the brunt of someone's joke. He was wildly popular at the Turkish Village, the one individual visitors remembered and talked about.

Photographers immortalized those along the Midway whom they found interesting in appearance or in their performances. This unnamed gentleman was one of the Wild East Bedouin performers.

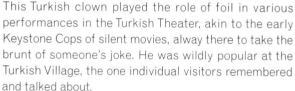

dinary wheelchairs of the exposition grounds which, with their student attendants, have thus far proved dangerous." The wheelchairs the reporter mentioned were just that, a fleet pushed about by college students on summer break, charging by the hour or even the full day, to a destination chosen by the weary fairgoer or on a guided tour (for an additional charge). Apparently some riders felt the young attendants provided speed at the sacrifice of a smooth ride although "dangerous" was an exaggeration, as no injuries or accidents were reported.

The portion of the Turkish Village running along the southern edge of the Midway street contained three separate structures: the Turkish Restaurant toward the west, a smaller and more informal café on the east end, and in between the Bedouin Encampment, known as the "Wild East." It is quite possible that "Wild East" was

selected as the promotional name for the Bedouin performance to mimic Buffalo Bill's "Wild West," a popular show just down the block and outside the official fairgrounds. Some three hundred Bedouins lived in tents within the walls of the Wild East concession, but it was the showmanship that people came to see rather than the lifestyle of the desert nomadic people. The Bedouins put on a superb riding show featuring sixty Arabian horses and twenty-two camels, punctuated with mock battles. Bedouin riders flew around the dirt arena on what many said were the finest Arabian horses they had ever seen. Also on display were the talents of the riders in mock battles staged on camelback. "It was great fun and the horsemanship was fine!" said diarist Jessie Wilson.

While the Wild East was part of the Turkish Village, it operated independently, and at

Far Away Moses turned up in photos constantly, here in the Turkish Village. He was one of the in-demand—and omnipresent—figures on the Midway. His popularity was due in great part to his storytelling and his eagerness to talk with visitors, and he seemed to be held in esteem by his colleagues in the various Middle Eastern villages as well. His face materializes regularly in Midway photographs.

This Turkish Oriental Odeon Theater performer is dressed as a shepherd. The Odeon was the main attraction at the Turkish concession and could seat fifteen hundred for each performance by the cast of sixty-five male and female actors.

a twenty-five-cent admission, the Wild East Show entertained nearly two hundred thousand people during the fair. Some publications noted that the Wild East show moved to the far west of the Midway, formerly the nursery and temporary housing for military troops parading on the main grounds. The expanded grounds would have provided more space for the Bedouins' elaborate horse- and camel-mounted battles that were a crowd favorite on the Midway.

At the back of the Turkish Village, in a corner that abutted the south wall of the Midway (behind which ran the railroad tracks) at the south edge of the Woodlawn Street viaduct was the Persian Tent or Persian Village.

Even though fifty separate concessions operated on the Midway, the Persian Village, like virtually every one of the fifty, had excellent street visibility from one side of the Midway or the other. And few fairgoers would have imagined that there were "only" fifty concessions, since there were so many attractions, restaurants, and booths within each concession—from a few to up to more than one hundred in Cairo Street.

The Persian structure was nearly one hundred feet long and three stories high, with two towering minarets and a rather bulbous dome. The first two stories resembled a very ordinary boxlike building, but the third story was divided into segments of varying heights and appearances. Signs outside advertised a theater and "dancing girls . . . awarded prize of beauty in Paris in 1889." Hubert Bancroft described the Persians as offering "entertainment of questionable character." There was a consensus among

Bedouin warriors pose for the camera while practicing for the Wild East show, which featured mock battles and exhibitions of riding on Arabian steeds. In this group, each of the participants is armed for battle, and while most perform on horseback, the rider at the rear, with sword raised and seated higher than the others, is on a camel.

reporters, *not* echoed by most visitors, that the many practitioners of the art of belly dancing along the Midway were simply too risqué. The dance form was new to most Americans but did not want for an audience (of both men and women) in various locations along the Midway. Bancroft went on to describe other shows offered by the Persians as a "theater [with] a troop of men supply[ing] the amusements, performing in a small pit, where magicians thrust knives and swords into various portions of the body, and athletes, tall and swarthy, swung clubs and wrestled." His descriptions were always colorful but often lacked enough detail for readers to comprehend or imagine exactly what was being described.

There were also booths inside the Persian building where artisans sold a variety of wares, including gemstones, with a cutter on-site to provide exactly what any customer might require. Not surprisingly, many Persian rugs of all sizes were for sale as well.

Swordsmen might well have been the most prevalent entertainment on the Midway, with various performances from Bedouins, Turks, Egyptians, Syrians, and others.

Not all of the Middle Eastern dancers on the Midway were "belly" dancers; all types of native dances were performed from Turkey, Palestine, Egypt, Syria, Algeria, Tunisia, and other countries. Villages from outside the Northern Africa–Middle East region performed traditional dances as well, from such diverse nations as Germany, Austria, Lapland, and literally two dozen more when including the young women from the Congress on Beauty.

This popular dancer is Rosa, who performed in the Turkish Village.

The Persian concession, while limited to "just" the single building, recorded sales of goods and entertainment of more than $100,000. Several cigar concessions operated here and throughout the fair, and each did a thriving business. (The cigar box label shown in plate 7 is one example of the many custom-branded cigars manufactured for the fair.) One booth in the Persian concession, operated by Mr. Lee Cahn, sold "cigars and smoking accessories" and generated an additional $61,000 for his separate concession within the Turkish Village.

The list of items sold as souvenirs at the fair was ridiculously long. Throughout the fair visitors could buy "official" souvenirs that were linked to one another mostly by having the fair's name on the item, a practice that has never wavered over the years at expositions. But many souvenirs—china, medals, glasses, paperweights, and so on—featured pictures of buildings or of Columbus. The most popular souvenirs on the Midway, however, were native arts and crafts from around the world; in the Turkish Village visitors could purchase historical swords and weapons, tapestries, furniture, housewares, and many other items—even the "priceless" silver bed was for sale!

Besides the principal theatrical production, visitors to the Persian village also could view "comedy and tragedy, oriental weddings, dances, funerals, merry-making, battles and scenes from every phase of life." The fact that the performances were in either Turkish or Arabic did not seem to deter fairgoers, as the Turkish Village and its entertainment were among the most popular on the Midway.

In addition, there was a row of thirteen small structures within the Persian Village, each staffed by Middle Eastern artists who were carving, weaving, or metalworking—and selling their goods as they were created.

The Turkish Village was one of the most popular, and most profitable, sites on the Midway, generating nearly $500,000 from the various enterprises. At one point Sol Bloom's Algerian concession exhausted its stock of the souvenirs they had brought with them, so they purchased a variety of handmade slippers and embroideries from the Turkish Village and sold them in the Algerian store. There were no false pretenses; they did not present a one-dollar facsimile pretending to be a ten-dollar original or claim that the Turkish artwork was Algerian. It was simply one vendor purchasing wholesale from another in order to continue selling souvenirs, and a pair of handsome slippers made in Turkey and sold by Algerians was just the same to fairgoing souvenir collectors as virtually identical slippers made in Algeria and sold by Algerians.

Considering the immense variety of goods on the Midway and even the conglomeration being sold within each concession, it is highly unlikely that most shoppers ever knew, or cared, about the nation of origin of their purchases. Would anyone have been disturbed to discover that the colorful slippers purchased in the Algerian concession were actually made by an artisan from Constantinople? The items were all exotic and from countries surrounding the Mediterranean—and perhaps one such item remains in a display cabinet of the great-great-grandchildren of those shoppers. It may have an at-tached scrap of yellowed paper that notes, "Papa bought these on the Midway at the great fair in 1893." Today hundreds of different souvenirs from the World's Columbian Exposition are in collections around the world. Many are imprinted in some fashion with the year or the fair's name. But what of the slippers, rugs, goblets, brooches, and other souvenirs from concessions on the Midway made—and sold—by Egyptians, Javanese, Japanese, Chinese, Turkish, Germans, Algerians, and others? The best provenance we can hope for is a note or letter written in 1893 accompanying the item. Few of the remaining treasures have any printed documentation or story surviving to share, except perhaps "my great-aunt said she bought this in Chicago in 1893," while the vast majority might be dated by experts to the end of the nineteenth century but with no chance of being linked to the exposition or the Midway.

A Day in the Alps

One of the international offerings on the Midway was more a virtual tour than a chance for direct contact with the people and their crafts. Next door to the Turkish Village was a simple round structure that featured no souvenirs for sale nor performances by a native orchestra. The Panorama of the Bernese Alps took advantage of every bit of electrical and mechanical technology available at the time in an attempt to re-create the Swiss Alps "in motion" for its audiences. Fairgoers were very appreciative of the ambitious undertaking.

A panorama of the Alps, reaching to the ceiling of the building and more than five hundred feet long, formed the heart of the cyclorama theater. Viewers faced the stage and the concave wall of the building. The stage was fitted with supports for the gigantic roll of canvas. An overlay obscured much of the painted roll as it passed so the audience could see only a six-foot wide portion of the presentation at once. This six-foot gap was the "screen" on which they viewed the show. The movement of the canvas

The Panorama of the Bernese Alps, like many smaller concessions, invested heavily in its building. Most of the structures along the Midway, like those on the main grounds, gave no hint that they were temporary and would be dismantled, sold, or simply demolished after the six months of the fair.

was carefully synchronized with phonograph music, appropriate lighting, and cool temperatures (all electrically provided), gently transporting viewers from valleys of wildflowers to the rugged mountaintops, to rustic farms and picturesque villages. As the fifteen-minute journey moved from day to night, the vivid scenery included a flock of sheep, a herd of cows being driven along a winding roadway by a milkmaid, thunderstorms, sunrise and sunset, and finally moonrise and the stars. The phonograph made the experience complete with such sounds as the "baa" of the sheep, tinkling cowbells, and roars of thunder.

Admission to the little theater was twenty-five cents, and income was sorely limited compared to most concessions. In six months, some ninety thousand visitors took the journey through a day in the Alps. With two shows per hour daily for ten hours, the theater averaged only some twenty-five visitors per show. But one visitor wrote home that it was "wonderful," the best thing being not the colorful presentation but the "fifteen minutes of rest and cool temperatures." The summer heat was so oppressive in 1893 Chicago that a fifteen-minute respite from the sweltering heat was, to that visitor and likely many others, a far greater highlight than the show itself.

Natatorium

To the east of the Bernese Alps was a concession that was a bit of an anomaly, as it was intended to provide an oasis with more than just cooling fans in the midst of the summer heat. The Natatorium (indoor swimming pool) was the fourth one in the city at the time, a public spot for recreation. Swimmers would luxuriate in water piped in from Lake Michigan.

In addition to the pool and its "many kinds of bathing" (probably including a shallow spot for lounging and a larger area for swimming laps), the facility contained a bakery and lunch room and "a café/dining room where guests could enjoy any type of meal from light snack to full dinner." Old Vienna shared its dining expertise, operating a portion of the food service within the Natatorium. By the time the fair opened the café was just another successful restaurant on the fairgrounds, but the swimming facilities were never opened. Perhaps logic intervened: How many fairgoers, surrounded by the awe-inspiring grounds and all the excitement and variety available on the Midway, would stop, change clothes, and go for a swim in the middle of the day amid their world's fair adventure?

A mystery remains surrounding the Natatorium: tickets have been found (for fifty cents) for the "Natatorium Gymnase." Not listed in any guide, it probably was a portion of the facility that never opened. A single ticket has also been found for the rental of swimming trunks!

Besides the bakery, café, and dining room, the Natatorium also offered private dining rooms and a large outdoor terrace on which patrons could enjoy their meals if the midday sun was taking a brief hiatus.

Despite high revenues comparable to most other restaurants at the fair, the Natatorium operators said their venture failed to profit. It was essentially only a restaurant with no admission charge and no entertainment, yet the owners had invested substantially in the pool and related facilities, including building a pipeline to bring water from the lake to the Natatorium. Still, when full meals could be purchased for a half dollar, bakery items for much less, plus beverages, snacks, and even more elaborate dinners for a dollar or more, the Natatorium realized total sales of nearly $300,000 in six months—without any revenue from swimmers.

Johor, Java, and South Sea Villages

The Johor (misspelled *Johore* in literature at the exposition) Village was located between the Natatorium and the South Sea Islanders' facility. The Sultanate of Johor, with a total population of less than five hundred thousand in

1893, seemed an unlikely exhibitor; today the small state is one of the most highly developed in Malaysia and is home to more than three million residents. Abu Bakar (misspelled *Baker* in exposition literature), who had been Sultan of Johor for nearly thirty years at the time of the World's Columbian Exposition, has since been called the father of modern Johor for his development of a constitution and enabling the state's growth. Despite the small population of Johor in 1893, it was typical of Bakar's leadership to showcase his people and their agricultural products. Johor exhibited on the main grounds in the Agricultural Building and also built a village on the Midway with a teahouse and booths selling crafts and souvenirs.

The South Sea Islanders and Javanese together secured the large Midway frontage on the south and also a like-sized parcel across the street on the north; they were the only exhibitors with space on both sides of the street, seeing an opportunity to attract fairgoers from both sides of the street. They did, however, operate under separate concession contracts for financial purposes.

The population of the Java Village, one of both the largest (in square footage) and most successful (in revenue) on the Midway, was a bit smaller than some of the large villages, with a total of 135 Javanese living in the village during the fair.

The Javanese were often referred to as the "gentlest" of the foreign contingents, portrayed as a peaceful people with a calm and quiet nature. Music far quieter and more melodic than the Dahomeyans' was played in a bamboo-walled building that could hold an estimated one thousand visitors for each performance. An orchestra behind the stage consisted of a *rebab* or two-stringed violin that looked more like a harp; a *saeling* or bamboo whistle; *gambangs* and *sarangs*, both similar to xylophones; and the *bedoeg*, *gendang*, and *bonang*, bongs and drums of various types and sizes, some metal, some wood and rattan. The resulting music was reportedly soothing to the ear,

Java Village was quiet before the day's throngs entered the Midway. The man in the center, glancing to his left, *may be* a Columbian guard (members of the fair's police force were constantly in view, as much to assist fairgoers as to deter crime) or another uniformed fair employee. The uniform is difficult to identify at this distance.

Inside the Javanese Village, residents in their traditional garb pose for the camera—men, women, youths, and small children, all of whom lived in homes on the Midway virtually identical to those in Java.

The Java Theater performances featured actors and actresses in brightly colored costumes and masks that gave no indication of the gender or looks of those hidden behind them. These two young women, featured performers in the Java Theater, pose in their Native attire without their masks.

This is a view of the Java Village from across the Midway's center street. Beyond the village to the northeast is one of the brand-new hotels built in 1892 or 1893 just a short walk from the fairgrounds. While many fairgoers chose to stay in established hotels downtown (seven miles north of the Midway), tens of thousands preferred the new facilities surrounding the grounds.

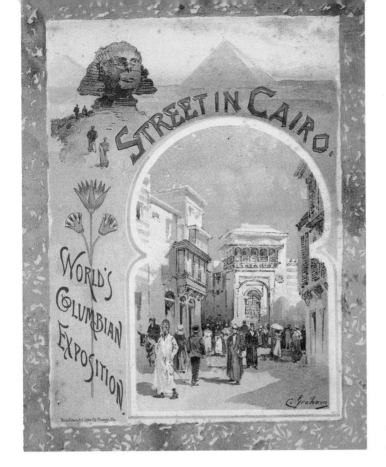

Plate 1. Charles Graham found dozens of opportunities to sell his work at the fair. His watercolors were used in newspapers and books and on the cover of the Street in Cairo brochure.

MIDWAY CHARACTER TYPES.

Plate 2. A term that would be offensive today but that was common in 1893 was "Midway Types." Writers and artists shared descriptions of the various "types" of people on the Midway. This view shows a Middle Eastern dancer and others of the "same type" watching.

Plate 3. Watercolor artist Charles Graham accurately portrayed many aspects of the Midway but took more than a few artistic liberties. The foreground of this painting, like many of his paintings, contained only a portion of what actually existed. The images of the tables and chairs are quite accurate, but the actual garden café and performance area contained seating for hundreds, possibly more than one thousand, in the open space where Graham shows only a handful of tables and chairs.

Plate 4. Charles Graham's extremely detailed watercolors appeared in more than twenty publications. Here he took minor liberties by widening the Midway and presenting an open expanse in front of the Ferris Wheel, where in fact the villages on the sides of the Plaisance had but a sixty-foot street between them.

VIEW FROM FERRIS WHEEL.

Plate 5. This Charles Graham view from the Ferris Wheel is an unusually simplistic painting for the artist, lacking the detail and ebullience of most of his Midway paintings. But this painting, like his others, found its way into the *Chicago Tribune* and also a portfolio of individual prints. The large boat heading south on Lake Michigan looks remarkably like a modern yacht as opposed to a vessel one would see in 1893.

Price 10 Cents.

Plate 6. The program from the Turkish Theater was singular of purpose compared to the many brochures promoting multiple aspects of other concessions. This was very clearly a program designed strictly to accompany the performance in the theater, a souvenir fairgoers could take home afterward.

Plate 7. There was no shortage of commercial products spawned by the fair. This is but one of several special brands of cigars introduced at the World's Columbian Exposition to capitalize on both the public's desire for cigars and its fascination with everything Columbian.

Plate 8. Charles Graham's evening pastoral painting of Blarney Castle and a single couple strolling a wooded pathway—a pathway conjured out of the artist's imagination. Seldom if ever could one find just two people strolling on an empty Midway unless it was after closing, when concession employees might be found alone under the stars.

Plate 9. Most of Charles Graham's paintings were "scenes" or overviews, such as this one of a single street inside the Cairo Concession. We would have had an even more comprehensive view of the Midway had he painted indoor scenes or those within the Midway's villages. Many small streets and alleyways snaked back and forth among multistory homes and stores.

Plate 10. Cairo Street and various other villages on the Midway featured both fully clad dancers and belly dancers with bare midriffs. As Sol Bloom reiterated, there was no single dancer known as Little Egypt at the fair, but there were dozens of dancers from throughout the world introducing fairgoers to the culture of the East. Painting by Charles Graham.

A group in the South Sea Islander Village poses for the photographer. The vast majority of the articles written about the South Sea Island contingent simply referred to them as "Samoans," possibly because most of those in the village were Samoan and possibly because writers could not distinguish the residents from one another.

and even the critical Bancroft found it pleasing, with its alternating metallic timbre and the tinkling sound of glass chimes in the wind.

The music was the background to elaborate plays the Javanese described as intended "to remind the people of the glorious past when the kings were absolute rulers, their courts were full of splendor, and when the gods were on speaking terms with the kings and heroes." Typically a Javanese play could last four or five days, but the Midway plays were shortened for visitors who might be willing—or able—to sit through no more than an hour or two.

In the teahouse visitors were offered, free of charge, coffee to drink and fresh coconut to sample.

More than forty small houses filled the Java Village, and wandering visitors absorbed the calm and unfamiliar lifestyle of the Javanese people. In one house a woman was weaving; in another a woman embroidered fancy appliqués

(both to affix to performers' costumes and to decorate slippers for sale); in others men and women wove grass hats, sewed clothing, made bamboo cigarette cases, and carved knives decorated with mythological figures, all for sale to fairgoers. In other houses workers pounded rice to be used for their meals, and a model builder made exacting tabletop replicas of the intricate bamboo bridges built in their native land. There were numerous houses for living quarters, including one for Prince Radhen Adnin Soekmadilaga and one for Klaas, the village's mascot, a huge orangutan from Sumatra. A popular attraction was the house in which several Javanese applied beeswax to fabric in patterns and then dyed the fabric (the dyes adhering to all but the waxed surface)—an introduction in America to the art of batik.

Java had come very close to missing out as a world's fair participant. Leigh Lynch, who managed the Oceanic Trading Company (OTC)

The Java Village was easily recognizable with its characteristic grass-woven wall and huts. A public restroom is at the left; besides the free toilets throughout the grounds—and comfort stations for women in various buildings—Chicago's Clow Sanitary Company had the exclusive contract for pay toilets and built "a nicer class" of facilities that, at a nickel fee, were used 6 million times during the fair.

and developed the South Sea Island exhibits for the fair, was also an honorary commissioner for the exposition, an appointment that was said to be political only and that gave him no authority. Nor was he given a seat on the World's Columbian Commission. He allegedly used his quasi-commission role to influence negotiations to obtain a concession under the OTC name. After doing so, he visited a variety of islands, including Samoa and Java, where he urged local leaders to send native people to Chicago and to build and operate a concession—which he allegedly controlled. A legal dispute arose well before the fair's opening centering on the fact that the Javanese expected to have their own exhibit *on the main grounds*, managed by Javanese businessmen. They had signed a contract with Lynch, believing that it accomplished their goals—and that he was empowered to provide such a concession to them. Instead, he had assigned the contract for the Javanese village to the OTC, meaning that all control would be under the South Sea Islanders' manager and that the Javanese would have little or no say in the collective village, which would be on the Midway, not the main grounds.

The Javanese took their dispute and their consternation with Lynch to world's fair management. Higinbotham mediated the dispute, and the Javanese, who were managed at the fair by G. F. C. Mundt, were able to create their own village. The 135 people in their village, all of whom were Muslim and built a mosque for their own use within their village, were able to build their concession without any interference by Lynch or others. Mundt acquiesced to Lynch, agreeing to pay him a commission (which he would have earned had he managed the village himself), and fair management assigned the Java Village an independent concession. Mundt told a reporter from the *Chicago Tribune* that he compromised financially in order to gain complete control, and that his people "came here not to make money, but to show what we had in Java and to try and bring about commercial relations."

Even with Mundt's acquiescence, the Java Village did very well financially. Sharing the site on the Plaisance with the OTC (known to others on the Midway and to visitors as the South Sea Islanders), the Java Village—totally under its own control—generated $155,000 in revenue, while the South Sea Islanders (consisting of eighty Polynesian Natives from Samoa, Fiji, Wallis Island, and "Romutah" (a misspelling of Rotuma Island that appeared in Conkey's official Midway guide) had gross receipts of only $93,000.

The physical space secured by Lynch was divided between the Javanese and the South Sea Islanders, giving the Javanese nearly three-fourths of the total ground. The Javanese buildings were constructed on wooden stilts raised seven feet off the ground, as was done in Java. Bancroft said this technique was meant "to protect against tigers, snakes and ants," which were no doubt of little concern in Chicago. Bancroft went on to note, as if it were noteworthy or different from other villages, that "the Java Village was always clean."

This program from the Java Village is still in its original condition, bound with a piece of blue twine. The program included a guide to the village's theatrical production and an essay on the people and economy of Java.

Inside the South Sea Islanders' village, men and women model their Native dress. The village consisted of people from several islands, but the press continually referred to them all as Samoans.

At the entrance to the South Sea Islands Village stood a large war canoe with a figurehead of a carved sea god; the canoe showed significant use "from hard service on the Pacific," according to Bancroft. The South Sea Islanders' enclosure consisted of four freestanding structures built of bread fruit tree wood. The village included a theater (admission was a quarter) in which songs and dances were performed and cultural items from the various islands were displayed, including several large canoes.

The South Sea Islanders' promotional manager was well aware of how to entice customers into his village. Just as the Dahomeyans used the word *cannibal* to alarm and intrigue fairgoers (though rumored to have been part of Dahomey's past, cannibalism was certainly absent in the late nineteenth century), the South Sea Islanders' theater was painted with Natives in various poses, a small bit of lettering that read "25 cents admission" and then along the top of the building in bold letters, "Songs and Feast Dances of the South Sea Islands . . . Samoan War Dances . . . Fiji Island Cannibal Dances."

On the north side of the Plaisance the Javanese also operated the Java Lunch Room, while on the south side were the Home Restaurant and the Bakery. The Java Lunch Room advertised itself as providing "the choicest home cooking, quick service and the lowest prices on the Plaisance." Whether they were, in fact, the lowest prices was a matter of interpretation and comparisons by the fairgoers, but the concession was both busy and profitable, with total food sales of more than $103,000.

Hagenbeck's Wild Animals

Just to the east of the South Sea Islanders on the south side of the Plaisance was the extremely popular Hagenbeck's Arena. In the nineteenth century, just as today, everyone seemed to love watching animals, whether they were cute or ferocious. This concession offered a variety of both. The Hagenbeck circus performances included lions, tigers, bears, elephants, dogs, parrots, and monkeys.

The Hagenbeck structure looked for the most part as if it belonged in the more permanent-appearing main grounds. The roof of the two-story building had gazebo-like turrets at the corners where guests could dine in a garden atmosphere. The center of the roof featured a three-story domelike design that provided a large open area above the forty-five-hundred-seat ring inside. The cast of characters was from Berlin, where Hagenbeck animal shows performed in their own permanent structure year-round.

There was an obvious air of commercial professionalism (as the cast was, indeed, very experienced) about the incredibly popular concession. There was no need to study Native peoples and cultures or to walk through villages: this was pure entertainment that Americans and foreigners alike could relate to better than many other attractions. Most everyone had seen or was familiar with circuses, and Hagenbeck's was an animal circus and showmanship at its best.

The Hagenbeck facility included two viewing options: Fairgoers could visit the animals at rest in their cages in a zoolike setting as well as view a wide variety of animal pictures and displays, all for a quarter. The actual show in the arena had three classes of seats, priced quite naturally by proximity to the ring—one dollar, seventy-five cents, and fifty cents. The dollar charge was surpassed on the Midway only by the two-dollar cost of a ride aloft in a hot air balloon.

The main attractions included a wire-walking bear, a dog and monkey riding Bengal tigers, a team of tigers pulling a chariot "manned" by a lion, and a lion riding a horse. One animal not required to perform but merely there to give a snort or two at the happy crowd was Lily, allegedly a dwarf elephant said to be just three feet tall, four and half feet long, and weighing only 155 pounds. The elephant was indeed quite small, but dwarf elephants had been thought to be extinct for tens of thousands of years. One was reportedly photographed in the wild in 2014;

Hagenbeck's Arena was perhaps the most recognizable concession to fairgoers. Circuslike in every aspect, Hagenbeck's was a German company with a well-established history of European performances year-round. The signs say it all: Lions on Horseback, Tigers on Velocipedes, Dwarf Elephant Lily. Inside, one could sit in an arena to watch the circus, wander around to look at the animals in their cages, visit a café, or sit down for a full meal at a restaurant.

Hagenbeck's souvenir program, which cost circus attendees ten cents, was "middle of the road" in style, size, and vibrance compared to other concessions. The designs of the various Midway programs varied dramatically. There are no figures available for the sale of programs at various performances, but we may assume that the quantity each concession sold was minimal. For fairgoers paying for—and valuing—a performance at ten cents, for example, paying an additional dime for a small souvenir program likely seemed extraneous if not extravagant. Hagenbeck charged significantly more for his shows, so perhaps those sitting in the dollar seats may have been more inclined to purchase a small program than would others along the Plaisance.

it was five feet tall and estimated to weigh at least three times Lily's stated weight. Whether a few dwarf elephants existed in the late nineteenth century and Hagenbeck's team had one is debatable. Even newborn elephants generally weigh from 150 to more than 200 pounds. Whatever the pride of Hagenbeck's and the favorite of crowds was, she clearly was smaller than a full-size elephant . . . and not extinct.

Regardless of Lily's pedigree, the fairgoers loved her and Hagenbeck's, where the combined revenue from the restaurant, the café, and the several shows daily, seven days a week, was well over half a million dollars. This revenue was surpassed on the Midway only by Cairo Street ($788,000) and the Ferris Wheel ($733,000). A conservative conversion to present dollars indicates that Hagenbeck had sales revenue equivalent to more than $12.5 million, Cairo Street a rather astounding $19.7 million, and the Ferris Wheel $18.3 million in today's terms—revenue that would satisfy any concessionaire at a modern world's fair.

The team of trainers handled their charges nearly without incident through hundreds of performances until one misstep nearly cost a trainer her life. Heinrich Mehrman, the headliner for all of Hagenbeck's shows, took one night off and "relinquished the whip" to Marcella Berg, a relatively inexperienced trainer who was unfamiliar with the peculiarities and personalities of Hagenbeck's Bengal tigers.

She hesitated while attempting to hook a long leash to one tiger's collar, and the animal, clearly sensing her lack of control, attacked her when she hit him on the top of the head with her whip. He clamped his jaws on her leg just below the knee and was dragging her away when a group of trainers, assistants, and keepers managed to free her. Fortunately, the tiger did not bite down, which easily could have cost her the leg—or her life. Berg's wounds were superficial, but hundreds in the audience raced for the exits, and the *Chicago Tribune* noted that "women and children in the audience screamed and cried and three women fainted away."

Mr. Penje was a hero of the Midway as one of Hagenbeck's lion tamers. He was said to coerce a lion into obedience to "do tricks and obey orders as if he were a dog."

The East End of the Midway

Next door to Hagenbeck's, the only lion was one fashioned in glass on the front of the Venice Murano Glass building. The cost to enter the glassblowing factory was the very common admission charge of twenty-five cents. Thirty Venetian glassblowers worked on-site. The Venice Murano history dates from centuries before the world's fair. The Venetian glass artists, known for fine creations, developed the mosaic and miniature mosaic glass techniques seen at various world's fairs throughout the twentieth century and in brooches, bracelets, earrings, and pendants.

The company sold reproductions of famous historical glasswork and examples of the art for architectural decorations. They also offered cameos, plates, bowls, filigree, and lace designs and included semiprecious and precious stones

"Ye Olden Tyme" sign on the restaurant was but one name by which this building was known. The Old Time Restaurant was a log structure near the main grounds at the east end of the Midway. The concession was a "themed" restaurant ahead of its time, in that regard. It was decorated completely in colonial American decor with antiques from the period throughout the restaurant, and the food was advertised as authentic to the country's colonial period. Customers came via word of mouth and descriptions in guidebooks.

The diving exhibit on the Midway was more austere than most. It was a wood-frame building with a single large room and an aboveground tank where modern deep-water diving was demonstrated.

in their glass creations, among them sapphire, agate, topaz, jasper, amethyst, and various natural crystals and minerals. One of the main attractions to fairgoers was that they could select an item or style—including colors—and have it created on-site for them while they watched.

Whether by intent or luck (good or bad), just across the street from Venice Murano was the larger American-owned glass concession belonging to Libbey, which grossed almost ten times the revenue as Venice Murano. At all times fair management claimed absolute impartiality in concession placement, and both of the glass exhibitors may have thought that their neighboring locations would create more interest in the art, benefiting both vendors. Libbey's products, both blown and other glass, were dramatically different from Venice Murano's. The latter produced technical and artistic items, stained glass, mosaics, and small jewelry, while Libbey created dozens of different mementos of the fair and glass souvenirs. And both had the advantage of being just west of the railroad viaduct near an entrance to the fair.

Beautiful Murano jewelry made at the Columbian Exposition may still reside in the jewelry boxes of great-granddaughters and great-grandnieces of fairgoers. The exquisite designs and colorful miniatures made from bits of glass form amazing mosaics, and experts in antiquarian jewelry can determine which Murano pieces were made in the late nineteenth century, for example, rather than in the World War I era or later. But they cannot ascertain whether a piece was made in Italy or Chicago; like so many treasures from the fair, the glass creations carry provenance only in the stories of those who purchased them on the Midway.

Between the underpass and passage to the main grounds were three very different concessions in a cluster: the Submarine Diving exhibit, the Colonial Log Cabin Restaurant, and the Colorado Gold Mine.

The diving exhibit, which charged a modest ten-cent admission and hosted 180,000 fair visitors in six months, would be considered

mundane in contemporary terms, but in 1893 it was quite a novelty and a scientific advancement. A very large open area in its building featured what looked like a child's oversized aboveground swimming pool holding forty thousand gallons of water. The crowds huddled around the edges of the pool and watched as a diver in a full diving suit and metal helmet demonstrated the art of working underwater. The divers' solid metal suits and helmets were more like what today's salvage divers wear, as opposed to modern scuba gear. Such equipment was first used more than a century before the fair and had progressed through a series of improvements, so by 1893 there was little basic difference from today's diving suits. Few, if any, fairgoers had ever been exposed to underwater diving, however, so curiosity—and attendance—were high.

The Colonial Log Cabin Restaurant was exactly what its name implied. The cabin was built to resemble a colonial-era log structure, and the inside décor was from mid-eighteenth-century New England. The walls and displays were vintage American antiques more than a century old at the time of the fair, and the menu featured meals authentic to the Revolutionary War era.

Fairgoers were often confused trying to determine whether an exhibit or restaurant described in a guide—often different from one guide to another—was the same one on the Plaisance with a slightly or dramatically different name on a sign. In the case of the Log Cabin Restaurant, it was fortunate that one guide mentioned that it was operated by "Mrs. E. S. Brinton," since another listed Mrs. Brinton as the owner of "Ye Old Tyme Restaurant," and the sign on the building read "Ye Olden Tyme."

If the owner and operator were different individuals, the fair records might print only the person who signed the concession agreement, which was just as often the manager or operator as the owner. And guides often were arbitrary in selecting the owner, operator, or manager to list alongside the concession name. Thus, official records and guides to the Midway might list "Vienna Cafe" or "Tunisian Cafe" or, just as likely, "Rooftop Restaurant" or simply "Restaurant," all combining to make it difficult for the fairgoer to find a desired concession via any of the many guides—and equally as difficult to determine if the building facing them was the one they were seeking.

The last small exhibit in the shadow of the overpass was the Colorado Gold Mine, which demonstrated the methods of mining for gold in that state. The Rocky Mountain states had experienced a boom in mining in the midcentury. Gold was probably as much of a draw to fairgoers as the methods of extracting it. The concession charged a dime to enter and view the facsimile mine but offered no other attractions within the exhibit; still, more than thirty thousand people ventured inside each month of the fair for a peek at the operation—and more so to see actual gold. The precious metal was a highlight in many forms on the Midway, from the Colorado Gold Mine to the ornamentation and artwork of ancient Egypt.

Just under the railroad and before the Stony Avenue viaduct and that entrance to the main grounds were the free informational Adams Express concession, a small enclosure where "Bulgarian Curiosities" were sold, and one of the Midway's two major Irish exhibits, the Blarney Castle.

Blarney Castle

A reproduction of the original castle (which was built in the thirteenth century, destroyed, and then rebuilt), with a square tower stretching one hundred feet toward the Chicago sky, was the first dominant feature seen by everyone crossing under Stony Avenue from the main grounds. The tower of the castle ruins (plate 8) was the only part of the castle reproduced, but it was ringed by cottages and buildings on three sides, forming a castlelike square.

Among the houses and exhibits surrounding the castle were those showing Irish women at work as dairymaids, butter makers, linen embroiderers, lacemakers, and wool spinners. There also was a museum that included a variety of Irish antiquities, manuscripts, and art. And of course there was a facsimile of the Blarney Stone, available for kissing at no charge. The general public, however, was no doubt confused by the fact that just a few hundred yards to the west was another Irish concession.

Some reporters at the time claimed that there were two Irish exhibits not because of any discord regarding their exhibits or entertainment, but for purely political reasons, one favoring Irish home rule and one not; but there was nothing political in either exhibit, the closest being lectures in Blarney castle on the value of Irish industries.

If one were specifically interested in Ireland, while at the same time excited about the vast array of art, transportation, history, agriculture, new electrical discoveries, archaeology, and all the Midway had to offer, the conundrum of two different castlelike Irish exhibits was disconcerting. For no particular reason, many likely just selected one and skipped the other. Even with the high cost in time and money for travel, the average 1893 visitor from anywhere other than Chicago allocated at least two weeks to absorb all the fair had to offer. Compare this to an average visit to a twentieth-century fair, where the norm was usually to spend less than a week.

Chicagoans and those with the luxury of time and disposable income could do as Jessie Wilson did: take in just three or four exciting exhibits and shows in a day and spend ten to twelve days each month wandering the fairgrounds and the Midway.

No doubt time prevented a great many from seeing all that the world's fair and the Midway had to offer. Admission to the Great Buildings was all after the general fifty-cent fair admission fee to the grounds. The entrance turnstiles clicked some twenty-one million times for paid admissions, and another nearly seven million for complimentary visitors, fair staff, and concession and exhibit employees.

Most fairgoers either were confused or simply assumed that the two separated Irish concessions were one and the same—the Irish Village and Blarney Castle, and the Irish Industries and Donegal Castle.

On the Midway there were a great many features within villages, and several concessions did offer free admission. It is impossible to quantify the exact number of visitors to the Midway, just as no figures exist for those who visited main buildings, secondary exhibits, and the foreign and state buildings. For such venues, one could measure only general admissions and expenditures for paid entertainment and food. But even the most optimistic early estimates and revenue goals for the Plaisance were vastly outstripped by several hundred percent once the fair opened. Higinbotham reiterated many times that revenue from Midway villages in general and the Ferris Wheel specifically were responsible for the unexpected (and sorely needed) profitability of the entire World's Columbian Exposition.

Walking Back toward the West End of the Midway

Strolling across the Plaisance from Blarney Castle, or due west from the main grounds, vis-

itors would encounter two small commercial—and relatively inconsequential (to fairgoers)—concessions before seeing the confusing second Irish concession. Neither the Diamond Match Co. nor the Workingman's House charged admission. The Diamond Match Company was formed from a series of mergers and acquisitions a dozen years before the opening of the fair. The World's Columbian Exposition was held at a time of huge growth for Diamond, and its exhibit showed the public how matches were manufactured in the United States. The concession sold a small quantity of matches to visitors, but without an admission fee there is no record of the number of visitors. Likewise, we cannot ascertain how many people visited the adjacent Workingman's House, which was simply one of literally hundreds of free exhibits at the fair.

The Workingman's House offered an intriguing housing option to working-class fairgoers, who could see an example of a quality home affordable at their wages. The model house on display was identical to the houses that had

The World's Congress on Beauty presented forty women representing forty countries, each in a booth performing some type of craft native to their homeland. Many of the young women also participated in joint musical performances in the concession.

been built recently for more than one hundred thousand workers and their families in Philadelphia at a cost of $2,500 each (equivalent to roughly $62,500 in today's dollars), which the exhibit noted was "quite affordable for a man earning $500 per year."

In 1893, such a house was affordable and had much to offer. The model home had an interior space of 1,376 square feet, distributed equally between the first and second floors, and had seven rooms, including a bathroom. It also had a full basement. Quite indicative of the era, the parlor (living room) measured 18.5 by 9 feet, dramatically larger than any other space in the house. Also on the first floor were the dining room and kitchen, while the second story include two bedrooms, a sitting room, and the bathroom. The goal of the educational exhibit was to secure interest for a building program in Chicago like the one undertaken in Philadelphia.

Just beyond the Workingman's House was the enigmatic Congress on Beauty, also called the International Dress and Costume Exhibit. The large building housing the concession was divided into approximately forty booths, each of which was decorated and furnished appropriately for a designated country. In each booth a young woman, dressed in the customary clothing of her homeland, was performing a traditional trade from that country, such as sewing, embroidering, or weaving. Guidebooks pointed out that the "principal feature of the exhibit is the beauty of the young women selected with an eye to the charms of their faces and forms. The costumes worn by the young women are beautiful and costly."

This concession was the source of some later criticisms that not all Midway villagers and employees were actually from the native lands portrayed. We have no *evidence* that any performers and residents in the villages were from anywhere but the lands represented, but the rumors that some of the young women in the Congress on Beauty were American college students were probably true. The concessionaires' catalogs focused on the traditional character of the costumes and the exhibits and simply identified the young women as having been selected for their "charms" without mentioning nationality.

The Congress on Beauty also featured daily performances of a singing quartet and a dance group, the members of which were some of the young women representing each country.

Admission to the concession was twenty-five cents, and it had a total of 664,000 visitors. The marketing of this and every other concession was strongly geared to families, and the Congress on Beauty was in no way advertised with any risqué connotation.

Electric Scenic Theater

Just to the east and west of the railroad overpass were gates on the north and south where fairgoers could enter from the streets that dead-ended into the Midway. Upon entering, they could turn to the west to see all the Midway had to offer or head east past the Woman's Building into the main fairgrounds.

West of the overpass were public restrooms and the Electric Scenic Theater, which featured a *Day in the Alps*. Moderate confusion arose from the existence of two completely unrelated concessions with almost identical names and descriptions in guidebooks, the Day in the Alps and the Panorama of the Bernese Alps, both of which relied on significant use of colored lights, were housed in ornate, small buildings featuring paintings of the Alps, recorded sounds, and lighting that presented a serene and natural setting.

Arthur Schwartz, manager of the Electric Scenic Theater, had a second concession featuring tachyscopes (similar to nickelodeons), which was closely linked to another concessionaire, Eadweard Muybridge. Muybridge's zoopraxigraphic demon-

stration was similar to Schwartz's tachyscope demonstration. Muybridge met with Thomas Edison five years before the World's Columbian Exposition, and the tachyscope was a forerunner to Edison's development of the motion picture. The tachyscope had a wheel with images around the perimeter (similar conceptually to the zoopraxigraphic exhibition). The viewer peered into the opening, and as the wheel turned, the sequence of images simulated a moving picture. Schwartz placed his tachyscopes in the Electricity Building, where fairgoers had the opportunity to drop a nickel in the machine's slot and view a quasi-motion picture.

Program from the Panorama of the Swiss Alps, which provides very basic and generic information about Switzerland, allowing this publication to be printed in Switzerland before the fair.

The entertainment aspect was intriguing to some, but considering the millions who roamed the vast halls of the Electricity Building, surrounded by its thousands of free scientific exhibitions, the ninety-one thousand (or about five hundred per day) who invested a nickel to sample the tachyscopes was likely fewer than Schwartz anticipated.

Aztec Village

Next to the Electric Scenic Theater was a concession not noted on any maps or in guidebooks because it did not open until the last two months of the fair. The Aztec Village was in a stucco structure with drawings on the front to simulate early Aztec paintings. Entrance was through a roughly ten-foot-high arched doorway; admission was a dime to see "original home life and industries" of the Aztec people as well as singing and dancing performances. The concession reported gross income of little more than ten thousand dollars, presumably primarily from admissions, although the concession did sell a limited number of souvenirs. A very rare and beautiful pendant from the Aztec Village—an aluminum square with a corner pointed down, forming a diamond shape—featured intricate artwork and appeared to have been struck similarly to a high-quality medal. Over the years a very small number of these pendants have appeared in the marketplace, and it is unknown whether they were sold as souvenirs or possibly created as a some type of presentation or award piece. No other items or souvenirs associated with this concession have ever been identified.

The Aztec village on the Midway was small and simpler than most concessions, but it was not added until the fair was two-thirds over.

Libbey Glass Works

The Libbey Glass concession was one of the most successful along the Midway. Libbey even advertised that the entire factory building and contents on display were for sale and could be shipped to any location in the United States after the fair. The company apparently had no takers for its complete glass manufacturing facility, but sales of its line of souvenirs was brisk.

Libbey charged ten cents for admission, and each fairgoer received a ticket upon entering that could be redeemed for ten cents off any purchase. And Libbey was as vigorous as any concession on the Midway in offering a large and varied array of souvenirs.

Today, among the myriad exposition keepsakes available to collectors are more pieces from Libbey than from any other concession.

Libbey employed 275 sales and creative design and production staff at its concession. Just a few of the mementos available included a wide range of glass paperweights with fair scenes in either color or black and white showing through the glass from the back; spun glass attached to stick pins; vases, cups and saucers, drinking glasses, glass slippers, and more. Some of the most readily obtainable souvenirs (other than photographs and books) featuring the fair's name that are known and collected today are medals and glass objects from Libbey.

Libbey's building on the Midway was highly ornate, with twin fifty-foot towers on the front and an arched entrance topped with four-foot-high letters spelling "Libbey" and "American Cut Glass" around the sides. The top of the building was like a shallow inverted pie plate (looking like a very low dome) with a large

The Libbey Glass Company demonstrated all phases of glassblowing and manufacturing and sold spun pins and brooches, paperweights, glasses, vases, and other decorative items. The company advertised that the entire glass factory was for sale after the fair and could be moved and made operational at any site in the United States.

Two wheelchair attendants appear to be having a good time without any riders as they follow a sedan chair in front of the Libbey Glass factory.

GOOD FOR 15 CENTS

To apply upon a purchase. Two or more tickets cannot apply on the same article.

LIBBEY GLASS CO.
(OVER)

Libbey distributed ten-cent (and less frequently fifteen-cent) "rebate" tickets to those paying to enter the glass factory. As noted on the ticket, buyers could receive a rebate on the admission price when they purchased something at the Libbey store, where the variety of items sold was as great as or greater than any other concession.

chimney in the center that vented the gas furnaces used in manufacturing the glassware. The building was large enough to accommodate several thousand fairgoers at a time to watch glassblowers and demonstrations of the entire glassmaking process and, of course, to step up to the counters to purchase glass souvenirs.

Edward Libbey, founder of the company, had relocated the business to Toledo, Ohio, just prior to the fair and had just begun to be profitable when the Columbian Exposition was announced. He could have taken a spot in one of the Great Buildings, as did thousands of companies, but reportedly he wanted to be a part of the less formal—and what he thought to be more commercially viable—Midway, both to promote the company and to sell product. The decision could not have been more astute, as the Libbey Glass Works was one of the most financially successful businesses on the Plaisance—selling souvenirs, acquainting people with the corporate name and quality, and establishing much-needed retailers from around the country. The result was nearly half a million dollars in revenue on the Midway and

The Libbey Glass brochure seemed almost more fitting for one of the Middle Eastern concessions. The Libbey company was well attuned to marketing and capturing the interest of fairgoers.

the launch of the company as a major national glassware manufacturer in the coming century.

Donegal Castle

The second Irish village and castle were due west of Libbey Glass. The facsimile of Donegal Castle, like Blarney Castle, consisted of a single tower (a bit smaller than Blarney Castle at less than fifty feet in height) rather than an entire facsimile of the castle built in the thirteenth century. It, too, was surrounded by a group of one-story houses and cottages. This concession was sponsored by the ten-year-old Donegal Industrial Fund, which was dedicated to restoring and developing the small cottage industries of Ireland.

While those involved in the Irish concessions would have no doubt taken strong exception to being compared to one another, to the typical man or woman strolling the Midway, the art, lace, embroidery, Celtic art, wood carving, clothing, knitting, and jewelry here were indistinguishable from those of Blarney Castle. Both Blarney and Donegal Castles had large signs announcing IRISH VILLAGE, further confusing the issue for fairgoers.

Donegal Castle circulated a broadside that was quite attractive and drew fairgoers to its concession. It advertised itself as "Ireland's Representative Exhibit / Irish Art, Industry, His-

tory and Antiquity." It also promoted its two restaurants, the Tower Garden and the Donegal Castle Refreshment Garden. Admission to the castle and entire surroundings was a quarter, with no charge for any of the other performances or exhibits. No doubt listing some of the meals and snacks on the promotional piece whetted a few appetites along the way: Irish Stew for twenty-five cents and "Donegal Stir-about, with caramel and cream, 15 cents." The latter listing included no further description, leaving many to wonder if it was a dessert or perhaps a drink. (It was, in fact, porridge.) The restaurants served full lunch and dinner menus, including chops, cutlets, steaks, soups, and, of course, Guinness Stout.

Japanese Village

Adjacent to Donegal Castle was the Japanese Village, presenting at least a small amount of further confusion for the fairgoer. Guidebooks made it clear that this concession had no connection to the Japanese exhibitions on the main grounds and no connection to or endorsement from the Japanese fair commissioners. Despite this, many of the goods for sale in the Japanese Village were identical to those at Japanese exhibits on the main grounds.

The official Conkey guide to the fair noted that because of duty requirements, any pur-

This view of Donegal Castle and the Irish Village offers a glimpse into the realities of walking on the Midway—not just the attractions but a profusion of signs advertising the amenities inside, from food service to historical exhibits. One of many fire hydrants on the fairgrounds can be seen along the roadway in the center of the Midway.

Donegal Castle charged twenty-five cents admission to the concession and all its attractions. Many concessions did likewise, although others—especially the larger ones with many separate museums and performances—charged admission to the overall village and charged separately for admission to entertainment inside. This broadside describes the many educational and entertaining options within Donegal Castle, as well as opportunities for food and beverage (which always were charged for separately).

Expenses for a Trip to the World's Columbian Exposition and the Midway

One visitor from the East Coast of the United States kept a detailed diary of his expenses for what was a lengthy trip from his Delaware home, followed by two days at the World's Columbian Exposition. The expenses include a trip west by four persons from Delaware to Philadelphia to Detroit to Toledo and on to Chicago and two days at the fair for only two of the four people, leaving us to wonder why two of the party did not attend.

Trip West

4 berths in sleepers	8.00
4 breakfasts in cars	4.00
Lunch at Alliance	.80
Expenses at Mansfield	6.00
10 Meals and room at Toledo	6.00
Hotel Bill Detroit	12.00
Car Fare Toledo	.20
Car Fare Detroit	.20
Hotel Bill Toledo	4.00
Lunch at Mansfield	.80
Hotel Bill Canton	7.00
Railroad fare	12.00
Breakfast on train	4.00
Sleeping Car Berths	6.00
Dinner on train	4.00

2 Days Visiting the Fair

2 Shaves	.30
Beer	.10
Beer and lunch	.30
Car fare	.10
Beer while waiting	.10
Admittance to the fair	1.00
Irish Village	.40
Car fare from fair	.10
Eggs and sherry	.20
Breakfast	.70
Whiskey	.20
2 Beers	.10
Hotel	2.00
Coffee	.10
Coffee	.20
Breakfast	1.00
Fair Admittance	1.00
Postal cards	.25
Dinner	.70
Irish Village whiskey	.30
Cairo Street	.50
Cairo Street Dance	.50
Vienna Village	.50
Supper	.50
Beer in Chicago	.20
Room	1.50
Whiskey	.25
Breakfast	.60

chases visitors made from the Japanese exhibit in the Manufactures Building were required to be shipped, whereas items purchased on the Midway at the Japanese Village could be paid for on the spot and then taken immediately. The Japanese Village, populated by 106 men and women, included a variety of exhibits and decorations, and absolutely everything on display was for sale, including all the furniture and decorative art.

One diarist (who unfortunately named many of her friends and relatives but neglected to identify herself) looking at bolts of silk for sale watched as another woman inquired as to the price for a piece of silk out of which she intended to make a pillow. "It was $104 . . . and she BOUGHT it!" the diarist wrote. Although such extravagance was within reach for a very small number of fairgoers, the sale of very expensive items, including furniture, was not rare. Besides the silks, the Japanese Village sold porcelain, carved ivory, lacquer goods, cloisonné, bronze work, fans, toys, tea, shawls, bamboo, and beautiful Satsuma ware. The latter often had the fair's name painted on it, unlike most other items, and consequently such pieces

This view of the Midway could have been most any city street, with various concessions looking like typical city storefronts. The only giveaway here is the two costumed gentleman walking down the street on either side of the man in the suit; they could be from Old Vienna or the German Village.

can be identified today and are highly sought after among collectors. Prices for items in the village ranged from ten cents to several thousand dollars.

The village ran up to the Madison Avenue viaduct. Just on the other side of the overpass was the balance of the Javanese settlement.

Java Village (second side of street)

Catalogs drew no distinction between this portion of the Java Village and that on the other side of the Midway's center street. Visitors seeking information regarding which buildings and activities were on each side of the street would need to inquire or simply wander around. This layout was no doubt due to the conflict with the Oceanic Trading Company over the division of the secured concession sites; by the time the decision was made that Java would occupy both sides of the street, all literature had been printed designating each structure with a number and a description but not a specific location.

This section of the Midway contained many of the largest and busiest concessions. The north side of the Java Village stretched from the Madison Avenue viaduct to just past Monroe

Avenue, where it abutted the German Village, which in turn went all the way to the Woodlawn Avenue viaduct—nearly two city blocks. Beyond that was Cairo Street, which occupied a site from Woodlawn to half a block past Lexington Avenue.

German Village

The German Village occupied the largest Midway site in terms of square footage, and it rivaled Cairo Street in popularity, as evidenced by its crowds and revenue. To visit Germany on the Midway, one entered a re-creation of a medieval castle by walking over a drawbridge above a fifteen-foot-wide shallow moat. The site was patterned after a variety of German towns of the sixteenth and seventeenth centuries.

The village contained thirty-six separate buildings and storefronts, combining the look of the castle with that of a town square. Beyond the square were dwellings, including a fifteenth-century Black Forest farmhouse, and a complete farm with obligatory horses, pigs, cows, goats, and chickens. The village contained examples of houses from throughout Germany geographically and historically—Black Forest,

The German Village, just a portion of which is visible here, was the largest village on the Midway. One exterior wall seen here advertises the "typical" village. Inside, a variety of buildings range from a large restaurant and tavern to a city hall and numerous village homes.

There were two options for avoiding blistering feet from excessive walking. In front of the German Village, two sedan chair carriers take a fairgoer for a leisurely jaunt to another part of the grounds. The wooden box could accommodate two riders; the men carrying the sedan chair wore a canvas harness with loops around the poles, supported over their shoulders, supplemented by holding on to the pole with their hands. To their right, an attendant wheels his charge past a Columbian guard. The rolling chairs were charged by the hour, with the cost increasing dramatically if one needed to hire an attendant to do the pushing.

This folded brochure advertising the German Village was, as were most concession flyers and literature, printed in Chicago. Concessions did not have enough information on their layout and specific locations to print advertising and marketing materials in advance.

Westphalia, Upper Bavaria, and Spreewald, along with a Hessian town hall.

Upon entering the castle, one was surrounded by arms and armor to excess; the managers of the concession said it contained antique weapons and associated paraphernalia worth $2 million. The castle's design and weaponry conjured visions of medieval times. Interestingly, the

Germans were incorporated under the name German Ethnographic Exhibition of Berlin, and the principal displays in the ethnographic museum were the multitude of implements with which their ancestors could maim and kill their enemies. The fair's official guide described the Ethnographic Museum as "two large halls, one vestibule and a castle-chapel. The collection consists chiefly of implements of war and of the chase." But there were other examples of German art on display. One exhibit featured nearly one thousand examples of weaving and embroidery from throughout German history, spanning the period from the sixth to the eighteenth century. If reporters are to be believed, the arms and armament were the most popular exhibit at the village, however. *Exhibit* is the key word in that phrase: the restaurants featuring traditional German dishes and no shortage of beer were constantly crowded.

Once a visitor strolled through the castle and its arms collection, the change of scenery was dramatic, both physically and ethereally. The instant serenity of the alpine farms and villages presented a dramatic change. Had the Germans been able to build rolling hills and meadows, the transformation in the middle of the Midway would have been complete.

Around the town square were a city hall, a library, a museum featuring what the manager said was "the most famous collection of weapons ever gathered in Germany," numerous shops selling souvenirs and crafts, manufacturing of Germany (from sewing to making farm tools and implements), and of course the restaurants and beer garden.

The village contained a total of seven different restaurants and cafés, which the manager took great pride in saying were "acknowledged by press and public as the finest on the world's fair grounds, 'a Dream of the Rhine.'" While a reporter likely did refer to the village's restaurants as the finest on the grounds (and probably said the same of other restaurants on another day), the German Village could lay claim to a larger number of restaurants than the competing villages. Midway restaurants and the variety of foods from around the globe were routinely and enthusiastically praised by fairgoers and the media alike.

The largest crowds and the greatest expenditures were in the German Village's beer garden, and together the combined restaurants and cafés could seat up to seven thousand people simultaneously.

Two military bands played regularly each day indoors and outside in the Concert Garden courtyard. The Royal Prussian Music Director, Edward Ruscheweyh, led the German Guard Band, while trumpeter Mr. G. Herold led the German Garde du Corps Cavalry Band, ensuring a festive—and loud—atmosphere in the open courtyard, where the music could be heard blending with the myriad other sounds of the Midway.

Cairo Street

Visitors to the Midway walking to the west went from the German culture to one that could not be more dissimilar, that of the Street in Cairo (plate 9), which was arguably alive with more noise and activity than anywhere else on the Plaisance.

Cairo Street was said to be designed to approximate an amalgamation of "typical" streets in the city, and the similarity is remarkable whether one is viewing a photograph of Cairo in 1880, 1900, or 1920; the concession's designers were meticulous in re-creating their city, and to the visitor, Cairo looked no different decades before or after the fair.

George Pangalo, a bank manager who had lived in Cairo for ten years, first heard of the forthcoming Columbian Exposition in December 1890. The college-educated Pangalo was born in Turkey of Greek and English parents, and he was, without a doubt, entrepreneurial. He set about obtaining a concession at the fair as early as he could. Simultaneously he began seeking the sponsorship of not just any authority on Egyptian history, but one with whom he

Hawkers were a common sight outside Midway concessions, imploring passersby to stop and come inside. This fellow used the two-chair method to elevate himself above the street; others stood on a single chair on the ground or one placed on a platform. The contest was to be heard over the others and over the din along the Plaisance.

could work to ensure the government's blessing and the most realistic concession on the Midway. Max Herz, the architect in charge of the conservation of Arab and Islamic monuments in Cairo, agreed to lend his expertise to the concession's design and construction. He also obtained the blessing of Khedive Abbas II Hilmi, who could not formally sponsor the project but could—and did—provide a public voice in favor of it.

Perhaps the most interesting aspect of the construction, reflecting Pangalo's desire to be totally authentic, was his plan to have all the concession houses accurately portrayed with ornamental, latticelike *mashrabiya* wood balconies. Pangalo went on a personal mission to find houses in Cairo slated for demolition and homeowners willing to sell the woodwork off their homes. In at least one case, he purchased an entire home just to remove the *mashrabiya*. He went on to purchase other bits of woodwork

It appears that the women at left and men at right are lining up to await a performance. At the right, one of the men looks to be holding a photograph of perhaps a female performer—to ask for an autograph?

From across the Midway's central street, the front of Cairo Street and the towering minaret present an innocuous and deceptive appearance. Inside was a transformation from calm street to almost tumultuous euphoria as dancers, musicians, camels, donkeys, snake charmers, and performers of all types were around each narrow bend in the street.

Walking the Plaisance

A fairgoer awkwardly works his way up on a camel in Cairo Street along with a young boy, probably his son. Every time a visitor had a ride, a crowd gathered. They seem more interested in the man's maneuvering than in the other camels and donkeys in the area.

from inside and outside other homes, eventually obtaining parts of more than sixty-five Cairo residences to ship to Chicago.

Pangalo discovered early in the process that two other business concerns were attempting to contract with the world's fair for a concession representing Cairo. As soon as he learned of the competition, he incorporated his business under the name of the Egypt-Chicago Exposition Company Streets of Cairo and capitalized it with a quarter of a million U.S. dollars. His sincerity and desire to maintain accuracy and integrity impressed Herz and the khedive, and he further enhanced his standing when he assured the latter that the mosque in the concession would be strictly guarded and only for the use of Muslim prayers, not for tourists. Apparently a similar Cairo concession with a mosque at the 1889 Paris Universal Exposition was desecrated under religious law when non-Muslims were allowed inside to explore the sanctuary. While he was unaware at the time, other concessions were planning mosques that visitors likely would be allowed inside, alleviating any potential disappointment for anxious fairgoers who might be denied entrance to a portion of the Cairo concession.

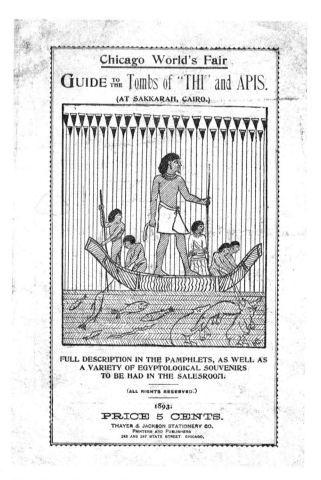

Cairo Street featured facsimiles of the tombs and mummies of Egyptian pharaohs, and this brochure was both a guide and a sales piece.

In the bright sunlight of Cairo Street, a young girl, looking somewhat apprehensive, is probably on the first donkey ride of her life. The Egyptian guide is on her left, and the woman to her right is likely her mother, dressed in a very unusual bright white dress. The style of the day was black or dark clothing, occasionally a dark print, but rarely the white both mother and daughter are wearing.

Cairo Street residents pray inside the Mosque within the concession. Not open to tourists, it was strictly for the religious use of Muslims at the fair. The Cairo Street management did, however, allow a photo to be taken.

Pangalo spread the word throughout Cairo, in businesses and among residents, that he was assembling entertainers, craftspeople, and families to occupy and perform in the village. He had no difficulty assembling the group, with the exception of female dancers. The dancers were reluctant at first to leave their positions in prominent Cairo dance halls, where they had worked for years to build their reputations and earnings.

Pangalo left Alexandria on the chartered British steamer *Guildhall* on March 9, 1892, with 175 men and women, 7 camels, 20 donkeys, assorted monkeys and snakes, four tents, a very large number of balconies, and a wide variety (and large volume) of other materials. The Plaisance version of Cairo Street was bustling every day of the week (with the exception of a few Sundays when the fair was closed), mirroring the crowds and frenetic pace of the actual city in Egypt. By the time Cairo Street was completed and the fair opened, the population of the village had doubled to 350.

This was the maze that was Cairo Street. Once visitors entered the "city," the narrow streets winding between the shops and other buildings were, more often than not, overflowing with visitors.

Whenever one entered Cairo Street from the street in the center of the Midway, the transformation was immediate, due in great part to the street's design. The street, winding past storefronts and residences, was always crowded and alive—Bancroft, every guidebook, Jessie Wilson, and visitors who sent letters and postcards to friends and relatives all agreed. Cairo Street was unequivocally the most ebullient location on the Midway, teeming with activity all day and into the night.

Cairo Street drew visitors through its arched entrance and distributed them along the streets of the city. Noise was constantly reverberating off the stuccolike walls of the cityscape, and the "bombardment" of the senses, one visitor said, made it impossible to discern exactly where sounds originated. At any given time one would pass camels and donkeys, some laden with supplies being taken to another part of the city, others with men, women, and children riding the animals for the first time. Dancers would clack castanets as they walked along on

unknown missions, and strolling musicians with unidentifiable horns and stringed instruments would be accompanied by loud drum playing on the many narrow streets of the concession and out along the Midway.

The activity level in Cairo Street was apparently so exciting and overwhelming that very few ever mentioned—or possibly even noticed—that the majority of the crowd surrounding them consisted of other gawking tourists just like themselves: dozens of Cairo residents and performers were surrounded by thousands of fairgoers from around the globe. Few noticed or mentioned the hordes of visitors crowding the street and seemed to see only the magical foreign performances.

Perhaps the greatest folklore originating from the Midway is the tale of Little Egypt, the ephemeral dancer who allegedly introduced the belly dance to the Western world. Throughout his life, Sol Bloom steadfastly maintained that no such *single* individual existed; no handbills, advertisements, or signs on the Midway ever

This Syrian Musician on Cairo Street is carrying a small ukelele or mandolin-like stringed instrument. Always part of the costume: a sword or knife, even for a musician. He is resting his right hand on the hilt of the blade tucked into his waistband.

Parades were commonplace on the Midway: mock weddings from Cairo Street, long processions of dignitaries, or simply gatherings of various performers from Midway villages, offering a free performance to fairgoers to entice them in for the rest of the show.

referred to a single individual performer with that stage name. In 1893 Chicago, Little Egypt was the amalgamation of literally dozens of women performing various Middle Eastern dances along the Midway, including the "Dans du Ventre" or belly dance (plate 10). Years after the fair, several dancers advertised themselves as *the* Little Egypt, but for six months in Chicago in 1893, Little Egypt was an apparition, while nameless dancers from Egypt, Syria, Lebanon, Turkey, Palestine, and other Middle Eastern countries undulating to the delight of visitors, created her myth.

More than one hundred booths, stands, and shops along the narrow alleys of Cairo Street offered myriad souvenirs for the fairgoer, including clothing, fabric, silver goods, jewelry of all types (and all prices), swords and knives, wood carvings, pipes, and assorted other merchandise. A two-story pavilion on a corner of the bending street had windows overlooking Cairo Street and the Midway where visitors could enjoy a bird's-eye view of the bustling Plaisance. The first floor featured a marble drinking fountain, open to any and all parched by the heat of the day.

Cairo Street admission was a quarter, although some hours of the day were free (and thus not incorporated into fair management's admission figures). There were also many ways to spend money once inside. One could pay for a musical performance, or for twenty-five cents visit a conjurer or a fortune-teller. Throughout Cairo Street there was no paucity of artisans—weavers, carvers, slipper makers, tent makers, candy makers, fez makers, tailors, jewelers, brass workers, and potters. There was even a public barbershop where fairgoers could have their beards or hair trimmed if they could not wait until their fair visit was over.

Theater seats for musical and dance performances ranged from twenty-five to seventy-five cents, depending on distance from the stage. The main performance theater was arranged with a semicircular stage facing the audience, with decorations as colorful and varied as most

85

everything along Cairo Street. An unusual element was that before and after their performances, dancers reclined on couches and massive pillows behind the dancer or dancers who were performing. They would sit and watch, clapping rhythmically as accompaniment to the dance and providing encouragement through cheering in their native tongue. The audience sat beneath a high ceiling with sparkling chandeliers, the walls surrounding them on three sides a combination of brightly colored drapes and fancy glasswork.

Snake charmers brought the fearful and fearless as close as they dared come while the ubiquitous cross-legged charmer swayed his pungi (the flutelike instrument made from a gourd) in front of a basket containing the snake. The charmers of Cairo Street reported that they brought nearly fifty snakes to the fair, ranging from six inches to seven feet in length and no doubt including numerous different species. They punctuated the act by handling numerous snakes simultaneously, delightfully scaring the audiences along the street.

But even the snakes of Cairo Street could not replace the camels as the most stimulating and entertaining animals of the Midway. Adults and children alike flocked around the animals who knelt, stood, and walked in their midst.

At the back (northwest) of Cairo Street was a Soudanese [*sic*] Encampment of nearly round huts with thatched roofs. Admission to the village was twenty-five cents. The chief entertainment there consisted of both mock battles with long-bladed swords and dancing by the female residents.

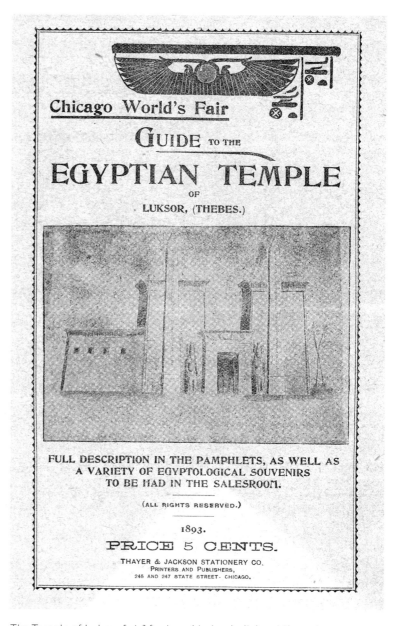

The Temple of Luksor [*sic*] featured twin obelisks at the entrance.

One of the most curious of the small businesses along the streets of Cairo was an operating bank, a tenant not otherwise affiliated with the Egyptian concession. The Northern Trust Bank established a branch primarily to provide a location for daily deposits of cash taken in by all the concessions on the Midway. The bank's main fair branch was located in the Administration Building and should any of the Midway concessions have found it more desirable on a given day, they could make their deposits there—a walk of some two miles along the Plaisance and through the main grounds. Pangalo's experience in banking no doubt was involved in Northern Trust's decision to place its Midway Branch inside the Cairo village. Northern Trust reported total deposits for the fair of $38 million, $1.9 million of which was cash handled at the Midway branch—obviously just a fraction of the money spent on the Plaisance.

Part of Cairo Street but sited along the Midway's main street was a replica of the ancient Temple of Luksor (Luxor). Its twin seventy-five-foot-tall obelisks towered over Cairo Street beside and behind it. Entrance to the great temple was twenty-five cents, while a tour of the shrine of (replica) mummies of Egyptian royalty cost an additional ten cents. The replicas included rulers from the Eleventh, Twelfth, Eighteenth, Nineteenth, and Twentieth Egyptian Dynasties; the highlights were the "remains" of Ramses II and III.

Souvenirs (advertised like many as "official") for sale within the tombs included items worthy of twenty-first century commercialism: scarabs imprinted with the world's fair name but written in hieroglyphics (fifty cents), a sphinx of Ramses II (thirty cents), and miniature obelisks like those at the front of the temple (thirty cents). Guides to the temple were available for five cents, photographic books showing views of the interior and exterior of the temple were seventy-five cents, and a history of inscriptions and hieroglyphics of importance in Egypt was fifty cents.

At the North Center of the Midway

Near the center of the north side of the Midway—between Cairo Street and the Moorish Palace—were several small concessions, including a model of the Eiffel Tower, the Persian Theater, the Panorama of Pompeii, and the Zoopraxigraphic Lecture Hall.

The model of the Eiffel Tower clearly was of more interest than the comparably and intricately constructed model of St. Peter's. The former drew nearly 135,000 visitors (more than five times as many as visited the latter) who paid twenty-five cents each to view the model of the centerpiece of the 1889 Paris Universal Exposition—and the iconic center of that city ever since.

The Eiffel Tower on display on the Midway was a one-fiftieth scale model of the original, and perhaps it was the overwhelming worldwide publicity and the recent construction of the Eiffel Tower that drew crowds to see the model on the Midway. It was set in a miniature garden of silk shrubs and flowers and lakes replete with miniature swans, all surrounded by exact scale bronze statuary. A thousand incandescent light bulbs from top to bottom were timed to go on at precise intervals so every visitor would be sure to see the Eiffel Tower with nighttime illumination. The tower was equipped with eight operating elevators that continuously took unseen miniature guests to the observation deck. The model was said to have been constructed precisely like the original, from approximately 650,000 individual pieces.

The Persian Theater, which was under the auspices of the Turkish Village, provided performances not unlike (to most visitors' eyes and ears) those in the Turkish, Egyptian (Cairo Street), and Algerian villages. The Persians also sold handmade Oriental rugs, swords, knives, and other wares made by those working at the fair.

The Panorama of Pompeii, like many of the exhibits on the Midway, created the illusion of motion (in this case volcanic eruptions) with lights and paintings to show the city of Pompeii before and after its destruction in the year 79 AD. Without actual photos of the exhibit it is difficult to know the extent of the miniature eruption; much about Pompeii already was known and some of it excavated by 1893, but the extensive archaeological digs and discoveries of the actual layouts of the public facilities, storefronts, residences, artwork, and architectural features did not occur until the twentieth century.

The Midway and main grounds stretch out on a hot and hazy day as seen from the top of the Ferris Wheel. The wheel casts a shadow over more than half the width of the Midway street below.

The fourth small (on the Midway, most "small" concessions were still substantial two-story buildings) concession in this line across from the Cairo Street entrance was the Zoopraxigraphic Lecture Hall, which was continually mislabeled in print as the "Zoopraxioptic" Hall. The Hall, located between the Persian Theater and the model of the Eiffel Tower, featured a presentation on locomotion captured by state-of-the-art electric camera shutters. When shown in quick succession, the images—like an old "flip book"—would simulate motion. This technique was described as the first realistic interpretation of motion captured with assembled still photography, since previously shutter speeds were not fast enough to capture images so close together.

At the Zoopraxigraphic Lecture Hall, attendees were shown a progression of animal movement through the use of multiple photographs taken one-tenth of a second apart and combined in dozens of images simulating motion. The feature included humans, horses, and other animals; running horses were the most often cited as the easiest motion to see by this method and the most realistic aspect of the demonstration.

Algeria and Tunis

Just to the northwest (adjacent to Cairo Street) was Sol Bloom's Algeria and Tunis concession. Bloom said in his autobiography that once he was able to secure temporary lodging for the Algerians, who arrived early, they went about building their village earlier than many on the Midway. It worked to their advantage when fair management decided to allow the public access to the fair site in the year preceding the fair's opening. It began as a "help yourself" approach,

This is an unusual view on the Midway, and the angle can prove confusing even to those familiar with the various structures. The photographer was probably standing in front of the Vienna Café, the corner of which is at the right, specifically to take a photo of the Algerian concession. Out of the picture, to the right and beyond the center of the café, was the Ferris Wheel. Within just this one image three separate small structures can be seen. The smallest, next to the Algerian Theater, may be a ticket booth not being used. But in the center are two fancy stands similar to ones that pop up in various corners of many fair photos. They are kiosks selling beverages as well as some snack or fruit items. Beverage concessions were enormously successful, even selling their products for a penny to a nickel.

with many Chicagoans wandering through the main fairgrounds watching the intense construction, but soon as many as five thousand visitors were on-site each day.

By this time the fair was adequately self-contained and fenced at the perimeters, so it was relatively easy to begin selling twenty-five cent admission tickets. As the construction of the Algerian Village was generally further along than most, Bloom was able to charge admission and benefit from the heavy traffic for much of the year before the fair opened.

The Algerian Village occupied more than forty-six thousand square feet from the main Midway street back to the northern access road. Fronting the street, the main village building's exterior was covered with tile work and had minarets to the left and right. As with so many of the concessions, the Algeria and Tunis Village included a performance theater and a restaurant. Song and dance provided by each nationality were popular, and cold beverages were in huge demand (as in all kiosks and restaurants because of the relentless sun).

The Algerian entertainment (both music and dancing) was similar to that of many of the Middle Eastern villages on the Midway, especially to those who had never before experienced anything remotely similar. The theater at the Algeria and Tunis village seated approximately one thousand and featured an orchestra and dancing girls. In the streets were the obligatory snake charmers, jugglers, and men and women exhibiting their skills with scimitars and swords.

The bazaar featured a variety of tents and booths, outside the ornate main building, where visitors could watch artisans at work and pur-

A resident of the Algerian and Tunisian Village stops to pose in front of the Algerian Theater for a photographer.

This dancer from Algeria was complimented in the local press, despite the fact that she—like many others—performed undulating dances, some of them with a bare midriff.

This dancer performed in the Persian Palace, where some journalists said men were entranced and women offended by the "notorious dances" of the performers. Certainly by today's standards the dancing would hardly instill the "blear-eyed ecstasy" reported in 1893.

chase souvenirs and crafts. One corner also included a Bedouin tent where individual dancers performed. A theater in the large building was reserved for the troupe of musicians and dancers who had previously performed together at the 1889 Paris world's fair.

For sale were gems, jewelry manufactured on site, embroidered brocades, cushions, table covers, laces, perfumes, clothing, and even weaponry identical to those used by Algerian and Tunisian warriors but not sharpened to cutting edges.

Bancroft described the dancing girls, as he did those elsewhere on the Midway, noting that "one of the damsels steps forward and begins to dance, swaying her lithesome form in rhythmic fashion, at first slowly and then in accelerated measure. As the orchestra warms to its work her figure appears to tremble and undulate . . . agile and far more graceful than the pirouetting of a premiere [danseuse]."

Bancroft went on to say that the performers offered no "unseemly display of flesh," and that the performance was unlike anything most fairgoers had ever seen. The still unnamed belly dancing was performed to consistently large and appreciative crowds, including many women, but a small number of women did voice concerns that it was "inappropriate" and "unseemly."

The Algerian and Tunis Village was in the midrange of size along the Midway—smaller than the German, Java, Moorish, Cairo, and Old Vienna concessions, but comparable to Lapland and Dahomey among those that could be called ethnographic concessions. Bloom apparently had the right mix of talent and appeal in his concession, as it generated more than a quarter million dollars in revenue.

East Indian Curios

At the edge of the street, at a bit of an angle between Algeria and Tunis and the corner of the Vienna Café, was a small storefront featuring East Indian Curios, including inlaid metalwork, carpets, fabrics, sandalwood furniture, tapes-

The East Indian Palace was one of the physically smallest concessions on the Midway, appearing to be a part of the Algerian and Tunisian Village (which it was not), but the bazaar probably sold more per square foot than any other souvenir concession on the Midway.

tries, enameled jewelry, gold and silver jewelry, shawls, and embroidery. Generally none of the "stores" were referred to as such along the Midway but rather were called "bazaars," which seemed to offer a more ethnic connotation. East Indian Curios offered no entertainment or meal service; it was simply a bazaar, and it was as small as any freestanding business on the Plaisance. Competing with the myriad treasures available at the larger concessions, it still generated impressive sales of nearly one hundred thousand dollars from its multiple vendors.

Kilauea Volcano

Just to the west of the East Indian bazaar was the only statuary on the exterior of a Midway building, in sharp contrast to the main grounds.

A twenty-five-foot high statue of Pele, the goddess of fire, stood menacingly above the entrance to the Hawaiian Islands' Kilauea Volcano. Like the fair's Great Buildings and their statuary, it was built using the short-lived

The Hawaiian exhibit on the Midway was as elaborate as any. This polygonal building was filled with a single theater in the round, an enormous cyclorama of the eruption of the Kilauea volcano. The twenty-five-foot-high statue over the entrance was of Pele, the goddess of fire; it was created for the Hawaiians by a Chicago sculpture artist.

method of staff for the exterior (in the case of the Pele statue, over a wood base). When the buildings were whitewashed, they gave the fairgrounds its nickname of the White City, and few if any fairgoers were aware that the gilded statues they encountered on the grounds were actually painted staff.

The Hawaii building was polygonal, 140 feet in diameter and 60 feet high. Inside was a cyclorama stretching more than 400 feet around the building and reported to be 54 feet high, which must have been a slight exaggeration based on the appearance and estimated height of the building's exterior. The canvas was painstakingly painted with scenes of the islands and showed the active Kilauea Volcano erupting, with lava flows surrounding the scene. The audience was seated in the middle of a large room, as if in the center of the erupting volcano, while the canvas rotated around them.

Fireworks, multicolored incandescent bulbs, and the painting provided a view of the caldera and lava spilling from all sides of the volcano, punctuated with the release of smoke and thunderous noise booming through the building. The goal was to instill fear in the audience as they experienced the powerful realism of an eruption. The concession's promoter, Lorrin Thurston, told prospective visitors that "there are a few exhibits standing out from among the main, which no one can afford to miss. Such is the Volcano of Kilauea. The subject is one of the grandest on earth. The artistic treatment is of the highest quality. The mechanical ingenuity in creating the volcano and the fire effects, all that science, experience and money can produce." His comments, while puffery, were accurate if we can trust the reportedly enthusiastic reactions of those who viewed the entertainment— and who were often shouting in both shock and excitement at the thunderous rumbles accompanying the colorful spectacle.

Notwithstanding the robust fifty-cent admission cost for a single performance, 120,000 visitors paid for—and apparently were thrilled by—the creative production.

Sioux Tribes / American Indian Village

Next door to the west was the American Indian concession, which included members of several different Sioux tribes. As they had for centuries in the country's heartland, the Sioux built camps on the Midway where they lived, ate, cooked, and performed a variety of dances for fairgoers.

The battle of Little Big Horn, where General George Armstrong Custer and his men were all killed in 1876, and the massacre at Wounded Knee, where as many as three hundred Native Americans were killed in 1890, were both still of recent memory when the World's Columbian Exposition was held. The camp included displays of army and Indian artifacts collected from the Little Big Horn battle site. Both events involved the U.S. Seventh Army and the Sioux Nation. At the time of the fair, the idea that this land was first the home of the Sioux people, and that the U.S. government could have been wrong in both cases, was contrary to popular belief. There was speculation and concern before the fair opened that the Native Americans could still be thought of as enemies. There were, however, no incidents of any kind, and fairgoers viewed the Native Americans as they did those from Africa and the Far and Middle East—as intellectual and social curiosities.

Just beyond the Indian encampment was a second Sioux exhibit, the cabin that was said to

Two members of the Sioux Nation were photographed while relaxing away from their concession. The American Indian Village included members of various Sioux tribes.

have belonged to Sitting Bull, which was reconstructed on the Midway. Both concessions were decorated with Native American art, clothing, beadwork, hides, and axes, bows and arrows, and war hammers.

Rain-in-the-Face, at the time generally acknowledged as the Sioux warrior who killed Custer, was in residence and was treated not with disdain, but rather surprisingly as somewhat of a folk hero or celebrity. Despite many accounts by Native Americans involved in the battle reporting that Custer was killed by numerous gunshots, in 1893, seventeen years later, Rain-in-the-Face was still recognized as the man who *personally* killed the arrogant Civil War hero.

Rain-in-the-Face, who had been a young warrior at Little Big Horn, told his complete story to a part-Sioux writer, Charles Eastman, who published it for the first time for the American public. "Many lies have been told of me," Rain-in-the-Face said.

> Some say that I killed the Chief [Custer], and others that I cut out the heart of his brother [Tom Custer] because he had caused me to be imprisoned [earlier, when the army arrested many Native warriors]. Why, in that fight the excitement was so great that we scarcely recognized our nearest friends! Everything was done like lightning. After the battle we young men were chasing horses all over the prairie, while the old men and women plundered the bodies; and if any mutilating was done, it was by the old men.
>
> I have lived peaceably ever since we came upon the reservation. No one can say that Rain-in-the-Face has broken the rules of the Great Father [the U.S. president]. I fought for my people and my country. When we were conquered I remained silent, as a warrior should.

Rain-in-the-Face was reportedly treated with both respect and curiosity on the Midway, never with any open disdain.

Between the two Sioux locations at the northwest of the Midway were the Chinese Village and the Captive Balloon.

Food and beverage kiosks were scattered liberally around the main grounds and the Midway. These businesses were not shown on any guides or maps for a variety of logistical reasons, but they were popular stops for tens of thousands of fairgoers every day for biscuits, fruits, cider, soda, and more.

Chinese Village

The Chinese Village, incorporated for the fair as the Wah Mee Exposition Company, advertised that "everything here is shown just as it is in China." The main building in the village was fifteen thousand square feet on each floor and stretched up eighty feet in two towers at the left and right of the entrance, with eight tiers of balconied structure topped by bell-shaped roofs, patterned precisely after the architecture and colors of traditional Chinese design. The religious Joss House, elaborate in gold and red paint, was used as a house of worship by the Chinese, who opened it to visitors so that they could see—and understand in part—how the Chinese worshipped. There was an admission fee of twenty-five cents to enter the Joss House, the same amount charged to view performances in the Chinese theater.

The theater featured elaborate stage productions telling long, involved stories that might stretch into many performances before the entire tale was told. No women performed in the productions; male actors dressed in traditional female clothes, makeup, and wigs to play female parts.

The Wah Mee exhibit from China included this Joss House of worship, one of myriad examples of spirituality along the Midway. It was wildly ornate and a significant curiosity to fairgoers, who were charged admission to walk through and observe the sacred facility. The mosque in Cairo Street, in contrast, was closed to the public and was used only for prayers by the Midway's Muslim population.

The Chinese Village included a bazaar where visitors could purchase silks, clothing, jewelry, and a host of other items from China. The concession also included a tea garden and café.

By far the greatest revenue for all of the fair's concessions came from restaurants, cafés, and food and drink kiosks. Fairgoers were anxious to sample international cuisine, and the flow of Lake Michigan and mineral water was constant, as were sodas, ciders, and iced drinks all attempting to hydrate the parched summer crowds.

Captive Balloon

The Captive Balloon adjacent to the Chinese Village was a huge curiosity and also a very successful, busy enterprise at the beginning of the fair. The hot-air balloon was tethered in the middle of a large field within the boundaries of the concession at the west end of the Midway. The two-story building in the Captive Balloon Park served the needs of the balloon's crew and contained offices, staff, supplies, and, as was typical, a restaurant. There was also a theater for vaudeville and music performances. Admission to the park was a quarter, not including a ride aloft in the balloon. The Captive Balloon was the most expensive attraction at the entire fair, including the main grounds. The leisurely float above the Plaisance cost riders $2.00 each—four times the cost of fair admission or a ride on the Ferris Wheel. Up to twenty people could ride with the balloon's captain at one time.

A ride was reported to take visitors aloft to a height of either 1492 or 1893 feet. It was com-

The Captive Balloon is aloft with only the captain and one other person . . . an unusually quiet day on the Plaisance.

The tethered Captive Balloon can be seen just above the Chinese concession. The small structure at the right is a very austere public restroom, unlike the Clow Sanitary Company's pay toilets, which served millions of guests in what was described as a cleaner and more welcoming environment.

Looking over the pathways of Wooded Island (on its less wooden western shore), the lagoon, and the Horticulture Building toward the Midway. The Captive Balloon is just to the left of the Ferris Wheel, at only about 20 percent of its target height.

pletely operational as any hot-air balloon, but it was kept securely tied to the ground as it rose, the rope playing out until the balloon was high above the grounds, providing an unparalleled view of the Midway, the main fairgrounds, and the surrounding landscape. If the view from some 250 feet above the Midway was spectacular for Ferris Wheel riders who could see the entire grounds, Lake Michigan, and parts of Indiana, the Captive Balloon provided an even more dramatic and unique vista for those who could afford the cash and the daring to venture a third of a mile into the clear blue sky.

Midway through the fair, a rain- and windstorm ripped through the fairgrounds, and its major casualty was the captive balloon. The balloon was torn apart (no one was injured), abruptly ending the placid journeys above the Midway.

The West End of the Midway

At the Brazilian Concert Hall, also at the west end of the Midway, thirteen performers provided a variety of traditional dances. The Brazilians also had storefronts in which Native jewelry (most using feathers and shells) was

sold. There was also a stand selling cigarettes from the South American country, tobacco being almost as popular along the Midway as cold drinks! Cigarettes, and all the more so ci-

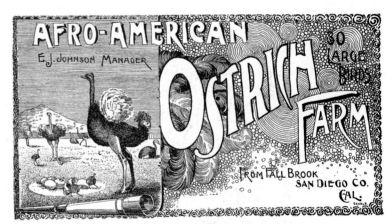

Animals, whether circus performers at Hagenbeck's or seven-foot-tall ostriches wandering in their large enclosure near the west end of the Midway, were always high on fairgoers' "must see" lists.

An austere enclosure did not deter the multitudes from the Fallbrook, California, exhibit of the planet's largest birds. The ostriches, like the Laps' reindeer, drew fairgoers in amazing numbers. The giant African flightless birds could be passive or aggressive but were always curious. A fairgoer was as likely to be ignored as to be followed around by an intense stare preceding a wild thrust of the beak to "attack" a hat, button, or purse for no apparent reason.

gars, were sold up and down the Midway and throughout the main grounds. Especially popular were the acclaimed cigars and cigarettes sold in the Turkish Village.

Just beyond the Brazilian Concert Hall near the end of the street was the Blue Grotto of Capri, a facsimile of the natural grotto created on the Midway with a mass of rock said to be 100 feet by 175 feet by 150 feet high; however, the thousands of photos of the fairgrounds and the Midway reveal that the height—and probably the entire size—was exaggerated. At 150 feet high it would have towered over all of the Midway except for the Ferris Wheel. The tallest minarets, towers, and domes along the Plaisance were no more than 100 feet high, and each was taller than the Blue Grotto concession.

Inside the rock structure was a deep pool of water artificially colored a rich blue. A mechanical "wave machine" was used to simulate the wave action of the natural seawater ebbing and flowing into the grotto on the Island of Capri. Capri has been a resort since Roman times, but the Grotto itself was not discovered until earlier in the nineteenth century, whereupon it became an instant tourist destination.

Likewise, the artificial grotto, with its rhythmic wave action and deep-sapphire-colored water, was entrancing to visitors.

At the northwest end of the Midway, the final exhibit/concession was almost as unusual as the Native peoples from other parts of the world. The Afro-American Ostrich Farm was—as was virtually everything on the Midway—designed to appeal to the curiosity of the fairgoer, and it did. The large fenced area featured a herd of thirty ostriches brought from Fallbrook, north of San Diego, California. For ten cents visitors could wander among the towering birds, touch them (at their own risk), and view incubators that would be hatching offspring from the gangly creatures who (at seven to nine feet tall) towered over all the inquisitive humans.

The concession was tremendously successful, generating more than $44,000—that is, welcoming 440,000 visitors at ten cents each. Ostrich eggs, presumably unfertilized examples for display, were also sold. Supply was quite limited, and the total revenue from the sale of eggs was only $500. There were no reports of customers boarding their trains after the fair with any ostrich hatchlings.

Epilogue

As quickly as the serene Midway boulevard was transformed into the manic Midway Plaisance of the exposition, the metamorphosis back to tranquility at the fair's close was even more rapid.

The buildings, villages, and kiosks were disassembled for use elsewhere or demolished almost instantly. As the denuded structural landscape disappeared, grass and foliage replaced it. Trees that had stood for decades—such as in the wooded area in the rear or north of the German Village—were suddenly exposed again and began to evoke memories of the Midway's natural tranquility of preceding decades.

Carriages appeared more often on the road between the new University of Chicago campus and the renaissance of the Midway. And seemingly overnight, two-seater motor cars began chugging alongside horses. By the end of the decade there was no hint of the Midway's ephemeral days as part of the fair. Today, it seems impossible that this expansive boulevard, which seems like the university's giant front lawn, could have accommodated—*could have been*—the bustling and crowded fair Midway of 1893.

The term *midway* became part of the American lexicon faster than *aspirin, elevator* . . . or *ferris wheel*! The dictionary defines a midway as "an area of sideshows, games of chance or skill, or other amusements *at a fair or exhibition*." And midways have been ubiquitous parts of our landscape ever since the close of the World's Columbian Exposition. Like the exhibits and technology of fairs, midways also evolved. As every aspect of expositions grew more sophisticated, so did midways.

Sol Bloom, the youthful impresario who saved both the Midway and the exposition's bottom line, had hardly reached his entrepreneurial zenith in 1893. He forged an empire as a publisher of sheet music, and then he turned his skills of negotiation, management, and creativity to public service in 1922 at the age of fifty-one. He ran for Congress and was reelected to fourteen consecutive terms, repre-

This rather sorry-looking image was taken a year after the fair closed, when the Ferris Wheel was combined with a vaudeville show on Chicago's Clark Street. The operator hoped to construct an entire amusement park around the Midway's centerpiece. Illustrating how fast technology and amusements change, interest in the Ferris Wheel went from overwhelming in 1893 to little more than indifference thereafter. George Ferris designed and built a wondrous rotating steel giant, but the world followed with ferris wheels of every conceivable size and type. Ferris's was the first, and perhaps the most elaborate, of all time; but the novelty no longer existed, in Chicago, or in St. Louis at the 1904 world's fair, where the original wheel was restored and erected . . . and by comparison to 1893, stirred much less interest and ridership.

senting New York in the U.S. Congress until his death in 1949. While in Congress he actively supported the formation of the United Nations and he chaired the celebration of the 1932 bicentennial of George Washington's birth. His autobiography devoted but a small portion of his life story to his role at the World's Columbian Exposition, significant yet subordinate to his years of public service.

In his retrospective view of the fair, Harlow Higinbotham wrote a final report to the Board of Directors of the World's Columbian Exposition in the form of a five-hundred-page book. It melded encyclopedic financial, employment, and visitorship data with his personal analysis of the event that dominated his life from 1890 to 1893. That Higinbotham was invested in the fair is a trivialization of the man's devotion to his job, to the city of Chicago, and to the legacy of the fair. Yet like Bloom, looking back, Higinbotham seems to see the fair and the Midway, while certainly significant, without the sharp edges and dominance it played in his life.

Higinbotham's writing conveys a sense of exhaustion with the fair, and his somewhat casual prose almost ignores or devalues the statistical portion of the report. It is as if he were writing to an only partially informed audience rather than to the board, which was intimately (often painfully) involved in the fair's ongoing details.

The following paragraphs from his report demonstrate the disconcerting, almost simplistic nature of Higinbotham's commentary on the Midway.

> Some portion of an Exposition must be assigned to light entertainment for the amusement of visitors. The eye and the mind need relief after the contemplation of vast exhibits of the results of human activity and triumphs of art. The Exposition grounds were most fortunately adapted to this purpose. The Midway Plaisance, a narrow strip of ground projecting at right angles to the west side of Jackson Park, offered an admirable location for picturesque displays characteristic of the customs of foreign and remote nations, and for various forms of amusement, refreshment, comfort, and rest, so grateful to those wearied with the exertion of sight-seeing.
>
> This narrow strip of land gave an opportunity for isolating these special features, thus preventing jarring contrasts between the beautiful buildings and grounds and the illimitable exhibits on the one hand, and the amusing, distracting, ludicrous, and noisy attractions of the "Midway." This strip had been abandoned

to the Committee on Ways and Means at the outset and it is safe to say that it did not occupy very much of the thought of the Exposition management outside of that committee until the time drew very near for opening the gates. During this time the entire plan of the Midway underwent many changes. Often the plat was completely filled up with concessions, only to see a number of them drop out and the substitution of others in their place.

Among the proposed features of the Midway, one most fully discussed was a "Bazaar of all Nations." This was a plan for the opening of a grand bazar for the sale of strange, interesting, and curious articles of all sorts and from all quarters of the world, India, China, Japan, the South Sea Islands, the Black Forest of Germany, Bulgaria and Roumania [*sic*], Spain, Morocco, Algeria, Egypt, Turkey, Persia, South America, and Mexico, in fact from every land from which curios and articles of vertu could be obtained. One of the results expected from this plan was the restriction of the sale of articles in connection with exhibits, so difficult to accomplish in expositions. The plan was attractive and might be successful at a future exposition. It was abandoned and the sale of curios was relegated to the several characteristic "villages" of foreign nations in the Midway. The articles sold, while generally interesting, were usually small and inexpensive, and there were fewer objects of rarity, great value, and artistic worth than could have been desired.

The first important characteristic concession granted was for a "Street in Cairo," conducted by the Egypt-Chicago Exposition Company. This was also one of the most successful of the concessions, the stockholders of the company realizing more than 100 per cent upon their investment. The admission fee was at first 10 cents, but the demand became so great that the fee was raised to 25 cents. The interior of the inclosure presented an interesting and credible representation of a Cairo street lined with dwellings, showing overhanging windows inclosed with quaintly carved lattices, shops for the sale of wares and curios in great variety, cafes, a mosque, a theater where dancing girls kept time to characteristic music, a fountain, etc. The street was filled with a motley throng of sight-seers, donkeys, camels with their Arab drivers, flower girls, dervishes, jugglers, sword players, and now and then was resplendent with all the glories of a wedding procession. It was vocal with the cries of vendors, the yells of camel-drivers, the shout of the riders, and the merry laughter of all bystanders. Probably no livelier or mirthful scene existed on the Midway, and few concessions were more popular or profitable.

That the Plaisance attractions added millions of dollars to the receipts of the Exposition at the gates, in addition to the revenue from the concessions, is certain . . . and without the Plaisance the great Exposition would have been somewhat less a complete whole than it was.

That Higinbotham seemed reserved and distant in his evaluation is odd considering his earlier effusiveness in stating that the Midway and the Ferris Wheel were financial saviors for the fair, a conclusion that is indisputable.

Bloom's legacy was indelible as part of the fair, his management in great part responsible for the millions of dollars contributed to the bottom line. And his statement of perhaps the most significance through it all? There was *no* single individual known as Little Egypt at the World's Columbian Exposition.

APPENDIX

Financial Data on Midway Concessions

Harlow Higinbotham often stated that his foremost mandate was profitability, and that the fair's *financial* legacy was that profitability was accomplished only through the Midway's success.

A brief overview of that success can be seen in the revenue generated by each concession on the Midway. The following tables provide this unique information in a variety of ways to help the reader digest the information. Tables are sorted by concession number, alphabetically by official concession name, by gross revenue, and by the amount of commission paid to the fair.

Following the tables are notes on the data and also a summary of concession attendance based on information provided in Higinbotham's final report. Only those concessions operating solely on the Midway are included.

Table 1. Midway Concessions Listed in Order by Concession Numbers

No.	Concession	Concessionaire	% to WCE	Total $ Revenue	$ to WCE (Gross)
1	Barre Sliding Railway	Barre Sliding RR Co (*did not operate*)	—	—	—
3	Turkish Village	Elia-Souhami, Sadullah & Co.	4.5%	474,602	21,274
4	Cairo Street	Egypt-Chicago Exposition Co.	20.2%	787,827	158,993
5	Home Restaurant	W. S. Troop & Co.	22.4%	103,695	23,215
7	German Village	Ulrich Jahn	19.6%	622,500	121,928
8	Natatorium	L. J. Kadish	24.7%	283,776	70,002
13	Moorish Palace	Columbian Moorish Palace Co.	25.0%	449,048	112,356
14	Panorama Bernese Alps	Benjamin Henneberg	33.3%	64,233	21,407
20	Dahomey Village	Xavier Pene	24.1%	113,153	27,288

Table 1. *Continued*

No.	Concession	Concessionaire	% to WCE	Total $ Revenue	$ to WCE (Gross)
24	Volcano Mt. Kilauea	Lorrin A. Thurston	33.3%	61,561	20,496
25	Libbey Glass Co.	Libbey Glass Co.	25.0%	490,322	122,583
28	Algerian Village	A. Sifico and E. Ganon	10.7%	257,660	27,457
31	Hungarian Café	Hungarian Café Co.	25.1%	50,611	12,684
33	Chinese Village	W. F. White	23.8%	64,207	15,288
38	Venice-Murano Co.	Venice-Murano Co.	10.2%	51,554	5,278
39	World's Fair Captive Balloon	World's Fair Captive Balloon Co.	25.6%	31,613	8,089
43	Blarney Castle	Irish Industries Association	48.7%	138,869	67,658
44	Diamond Matches	Diamond Match Co.	48.6%	804	391
48	Zoopraxigraphic Circus	Eadweard Muybridge	33.4%	320	107
51	Persian Exhibit	Elia-Souhami, Sadullah & Co.	20.1%	103,309	20,745
58	Ferris Wheel	George W. Ferris	28.9%	733,087	212,218
59	International Beauty Show	International Beauty Show Company	25.0%	166,021	41,508
61	Ice Railway	De La Vergne & Rankin	36.6%	67,319	24,665
69	Donegal Castle	Mrs. Alice M. Hart	42.5%	65,181	27,679
71	French Cider Press	Cottentin & Sieman	24.7%	9,001	2,220
75	Japanese Bazaar	Y. Maurai	20.0%	206,284	41,255
81	Vienna Café	Koenig & Greisser	26.2%	88,473	23,180
86	St. Peter's Cathedral Model	Ludovic de Spiridon	33.2%	5,958	1,976
87	Hagenbeck Zoological Arena	Hagenbeck Zoolog. Arena Company	25.0%	526,709	131,714
100	Tunisian Café	Amadee Maquaire	8.1%	54,050	4,352
102	German Restaurant	Franz Triacca	24.8%	333,561	82,768
116	South Sea Island Theater	Oceanic Trading Co.	25.4%	93,224	23,647
117	Model of the Eiffel Tower	C. du Pasquiere	29.9%	33,411	9,998
133	Lapland Village	Lapland Village Exhibition Co.	25.0%	63,716	15,929
137	Electric Scenic Theater	Arthur Schwartz	33.3%	22,898	7,633
138	Tachyscopes	Arthur Schwartz	33.3%	4,553	1,518
142	East Indian Wares	S. J. Tellery	10.0%	81,005	8,101
161	Brazilian Exhibit	A. P. de la Riberio	13.4%	11,669	2,917
172	East Indian Wares	Ardeshir & Byramji	10.0%	21,766	2,177
177	New England Log Cabin	Mrs. E. S. Brinton	25.0%	51,553	12,888
182	Old Vienna	Old Vienna at Chicago Co.	20.2%	485,702	98,349
204	Mosque of Tangiers	Jacob Benchetrit	25.0%	1,618	405
221	Submarine Diving	J. J. Mannion & Co.	25.0%	18,030	4,507
223	Ostrich Farm	A. J. Johnston	25.0%	44,826	11,206
224	Java Village	Java-Chicago Exposition Co.	29.9%	154,895	46,300
237	Panorama of Pompeii	G. Pandofelli	25.0%	19,506	4,876
238	Gold Mine	R. A. Campbell	25.0%	18,717	4,679
248	American Indian Village	T. R. Roddy	25.0%	24,208	6,052
253	Sitting Bull Log Cabin	P. B. Wickham	25.0%	10,564	2,641
257	Bedouin Camp	S. K. Bistanai	25.0%	47,218	11,804
288	Cider, Midway	Mrs. W. R. Robeson	25.0%	2,633	658
300	Aztec Village	P. B. Mills	25.0%	10,233	2,558
322	East Indian Curios	Princess J. Sorabji	25.1%	11,631	2,923
324	Cider on the Plaisance	Davis & Whitman	33.3%	17,682	5,893
326	Indian Curios	R. F. Hardy	25.2%	310	78
368	Ostrich Eggs	M. Berliner	25.0%	515	129

Table 2. Midway Concessions Listed Alphabetically by Concession Name

No.	Concession	Concessionaire	% to WCE	Total $ Revenue	$ to WCE (Gross)
28	Algerian Village	A. Sifico and E. Ganon	10.7%	257,660	27,457
248	American Indian Village	T. R. Roddy	25.0%	24,208	6,052
300	Aztec Village	P. B. Mills	25.0%	10,233	2,558
1	Barre Sliding Railway	Barre Sliding RR Co. (*did not operate*)	—	—	—
257	Bedouin Camp	S. K. Bistanai	25.0%	47,218	11,804
43	Blarney Castle	Irish Industries Association	48.7%	138,869	67,658
161	Brazilian Exhibit	A. P. de la Riberio	13.4%	11,669	2,917
4	Cairo Street	Egypt-Chicago Exposition Co.	20.2%	787,827	158,993
33	Chinese Village	W. F. White	23.8%	64,207	15,288
324	Cider on the Plaisance	Davis & Whitman	33.3%	17,682	5,893
288	Cider, Midway	Mrs. W. R. Robeson	25.0%	2,633	658
20	Dahomey Village	Xavier Pene	24.1%	113,153	27,288
44	Diamond Matches	Diamond Match Co.	48.6%	804	391
69	Donegal Castle	Mrs. Alice M. Hart	42.5%	65,181	27,679
322	East Indian Curios	Princess J. Sorabji	25.1%	11,631	2,923
142	East Indian Wares	S. J. Tellery	10.0%	81,005	8,101
172	East Indian Wares	Ardeshir & Byramji	10.0%	21,766	2,177
137	Electric Scenic Theater	Arthur Schwartz	33.3%	22,898	7,633
58	Ferris Wheel	George W. Ferris	28.9%	733,087	212,218
71	French Cider Press	Cottentin & Sieman	24.7%	9,001	2,220
102	German Restaurant	Franz Triacca	24.8%	333,561	82,768
7	German Village	Ulrich Jahn	19.6%	622,500	121,928
238	Gold Mine	R. A. Campbell	25.0%	18,717	4,679
87	Hagenbeck Zoological Arena	Hagenbeck Zoolog. Arena Company	25.0%	526,709	131,714
5	Home Restaurant	W. S. Troop & Co.	22.4%	103,695	23,215
31	Hungarian Café	Hungarian Café Co.	25.1%	50,611	12,684
61	Ice Railway	De La Vergne & Rankin	36.6%	67,319	24,665
326	Indian Curios	R. F. Hardy	25.2%	310	78
59	International Beauty Show	International Beauty Show Company	25.0%	166,021	41,508
75	Japanese Bazaar	Y. Maurai	20.0%	206,284	41,255
224	Java Village	Java-Chicago Exposition Co.	29.9%	154,895	46,300
133	Lapland Village	Lapland Village Exhibition Co.	25.0%	63,716	15,929
25	Libbey Glass Co.	Libbey Glass Co.	25.0%	490,322	122,583
117	Model of the Eiffel Tower	C. du Pasquiere	29.9%	33,411	9,998
13	Moorish Palace	Columbian Moorish Palace Co.	25.0%	449,048	112,356
204	Mosque of Tangiers	Jacob Benchetrit	25.0%	1,618	405
8	Natatorium	L. J. Kadish	24.7%	283,776	70,002
177	New England Log Cabin	Mrs. E. S. Brinton	25.0%	51,553	12,888
182	Old Vienna	Old Vienna at Chicago Co.	20.2%	485,702	98,349
368	Ostrich Eggs	M. Berliner	25.0%	515	129
223	Ostrich Farm	A. J. Johnston	25.0%	44,826	11,206
14	Panorama Bernese Alps	Benjamin Henneberg	33.3%	64,233	21,407
237	Panorama of Pompeii	G. Pandofelli	25.0%	19,506	4,876
51	Persian Exhibit	Elia-Souhami, Sadullah & Co.	20.1%	103,309	20,745
253	Sitting Bull Log Cabin	P. B. Wickham	25.0%	10,564	2,641
116	South Sea Island Theater	Oceanic Trading Co.	25.4%	93,224	23,647

Table 2. *Continued*

No.	Concession	Concessionaire	% to WCE	Total $ Revenue	$ to WCE (Gross)
86	St. Peter's Cathedral Model	Ludovic de Spiridon	33.2%	5,958	1,976
221	Submarine Diving	J. J. Mannion & Co.	25.0%	18,030	4,507
138	Tachyscopes	Arthur Schwartz	33.3%	4,553	1,518
100	Tunisian Café	Amadee Maquaire	8.1%	54,050	4,352
3	Turkish Village	Elia-Souhami, Sadullah & Co	4.5%	474,602	21,274
38	Venice-Murano Co.	Venice-Murano Co.	10.2%	51,554	5,278
81	Vienna Café	Koenig & Greisser	26.2%	88,473	23,180
24	Volcano Mt. Kilauea	Lorrin A. Thurston	33.3%	61,561	20,496
39	World's Fair Captive Balloon	World's Fair Captive Balloon Co.	25.6%	31,613	8,089
48	Zoopraxigraphic Circus	Eadweard Muybridge	33.4%	320	107

Table 3. Midway Concessions Listed in Order by Gross Revenue

No.	Concession	Concessionaire	% to WCE	Total $ Revenue	$ to WCE
4	Cairo Street	Egypt-Chicago Exposition Co.	20.2%	787,827	158,993
58	Ferris Wheel	George W. Ferris	28.9%	733,087	212,218
7	German Village	Ulrich Jahn	19.6%	622,500	121,928
87	Hagenbeck Zoological Arena	Hagenbeck Zoolog. Arena Company	25.0%	526,709	131,714
25	Libbey Glass Co.	Libbey Glass Co.	25.0%	490,322	122,583
182	Old Vienna	Old Vienna at Chicago Co.	20.2%	485,702	98,349
3	Turkish Village	Elia-Souhami, Sadullah & Co.	4.5%	474,602	21,274
13	Moorish Palace	Columbian Moorish Palace Co.	25.0%	449,048	112,356
102	German Restaurant	Franz Triacca	24.8%	333,561	82,768
8	Natatorium	L. J. Kadish	24.7%	283,776	70,002
28	Algerian Village	A. Sifico and E. Ganon	10.7%	257,660	27,457
75	Japanese Bazaar	Y. Maurai	20.0%	206,284	41,255
59	International Beauty Show	International Beauty Show Company	25.0%	166,021	41,508
224	Java Village	Java-Chicago Exposition Co.	29.9%	154,895	46,300
43	Blarney Castle	Irish Industries Association	48.7%	138,869	67,658
20	Dahomey Village	Xavier Pene	24.1%	113,153	27,288
5	Home Restaurant	W. S. Troop & Co.	22.4%	103,695	23,215
51	Persian Exhibit	Elia-Souhami, Sadullah & Co.	20.1%	103,309	20,745
116	South Sea Island Theater	Oceanic Trading Co.	25.4%	93,224	23,647
81	Vienna Café	Koenig & Greisser	26.2%	88,473	23,180
142	East Indian Wares	S. J. Tellery	10.0%	81,005	8,101
61	Ice Railway	De La Vergne & Rankin	36.6%	67,319	24,665
69	Donegal Castle	Mrs. Alice M. Hart	42.5%	65,181	27,679
14	Panorama Bernese Alps	Benjamin Henneberg	33.3%	64,233	21,407
33	Chinese Village	W. F. White	23.8%	64,207	15,288
133	Lapland Village	Lapland Village Exhibition Co.	25.0%	63,716	15,929
24	Volcano Mt. Kilauea	Lorrin A. Thurston	33.3%	61,561	20,496
100	Tunisian Café	Amadee Maquaire	8.1%	54,050	4,352
38	Venice-Murano Co.	Venice-Murano Co.	10.2%	51,554	5,278
177	New England Log Cabin	Mrs. E. S. Brinton	25.0%	51,553	12,888
31	Hungarian Café	Hungarian Café Co.	25.1%	50,611	12,684
257	Bedouin Camp	S. K. Bistanai	25.0%	47,218	11,804
223	Ostrich Farm	A. J. Johnston	25.0%	44,826	11,206

Table 3. *Continued*

No.	Concession	Concessionaire	% to WCE	Total $ Revenue	$ to WCE
117	Model of the Eiffel Tower	C. du Pasquiere	29.9%	33,411	9,998
39	World's Fair Captive Balloon	World's Fair Captive Balloon Co.	25.6%	31,613	8,089
248	American Indian Village	T. R. Roddy	25.0%	24,208	6,052
137	Electric Scenic Theater	Arthur Schwartz	33.3%	22,898	7,633
172	East Indian Wares	Ardeshir & Byramji	10.0%	21,766	2,177
237	Panorama of Pompeii	G. Pandofelli	25.0%	19,506	4,876
238	Gold Mine	R. A. Campbell	25.0%	18,717	4,679
221	Submarine Diving	J. J. Mannion & Co.	25.0%	18,030	4,507
324	Cider on the Plaisance	Davis & Whitman	33.3%	17,682	5,893
161	Brazilian Exhibit	A. P. de la Riberio	13.4%	11,669	2,917
322	East Indian Curios	Princess J. Sorabji	25.1%	11,631	2,923
253	Sitting Bull Log Cabin	P. B. Wickham	25.0%	10,564	2,641
300	Aztec Village	P. B. Mills	25.0%	10,233	2,558
71	French Cider Press	Cottentin & Sieman	24.7%	9,001	2,220
86	St. Peter's Cathedral Model	Ludovic de Spiridon	33.2%	5,958	1,976
138	Tachyscopes	Arthur Schwartz	33.3%	4,553	1,518
288	Cider, Midway	Mrs. W. R. Robeson	25.0%	2,633	658
204	Mosque of Tangiers	Jacob Benchetrit	25.0%	1,618	405
44	Diamond Match Co.	Diamond Match Co.	48.6%	804	391
368	Ostrich Eggs	M. Berliner	25.0%	515	129
48	Zoopraxigraphic Circus	Eadweard Muybridge	33.4%	320	107
326	Indian Curios	R. F. Hardy	25.2%	310	78
1	Barre Sliding Railway	Barre Sliding Railway Co.	—	—	—
	TOTALS		22.5%	7,444,522	1,672,761

Table 4. Midway Concessions Listed by Percentage of Revenue Paid to the WCE (before allowance of any claims)

No.	Concession	Concessionaire	% to WCE	Total $ Revenue	$ to WCE (Gross)
3	Turkish Village	Elia-Souhami, Sadullah & Co.	4.5%	474,602	21,274
100	Tunisian Café	Amadee Maquaire	8.1%	54,050	4,352
172	East Indian Wares	Ardeshir & Byramji	10.0%	21,766	2,177
142	East Indian Wares	S. J. Tellery	10.0%	81,005	8,101
38	Venice-Murano Co.	Venice-Murano Co.	10.2%	51,554	5,278
28	Algerian Village	A. Sifico and E. Ganon	10.7%	257,660	27,457
161	Brazilian Exhibit	A. P. de la Riberio	13.4%	11,669	2,917
7	German Village	Ulrich Jahn	19.6%	622,500	121,928
75	Japanese Bazaar	Y. Maurai	20.0%	206,284	41,255
51	Persian Exhibit	Elia-Souhami, Sadullah & Co.	20.1%	103,309	20,745
182	Old Vienna	Old Vienna at Chicago Co.	20.2%	485,702	98,349
4	Cairo Street	Egypt-Chicago Exposition Co.	20.2%	787,827	158,993
5	Home Restaurant	W. S. Troop & Co.	22.4%	103,695	23,215
33	Chinese Village	W. F. White	23.8%	64,207	15,288
20	Dahomey Village	Xavier Pene	24.1%	113,153	27,288
71	French Cider Press	Cottentin & Sieman	24.7%	9,001	2,220
8	Natatorium	L. J. Kadish	24.7%	283,776	70,002
102	German Restaurant	Franz Triacca	24.8%	333,561	82,768
368	Ostrich Eggs	M. Berliner	25.0%	515	129

Table 4. *Continued*

No.	Concession	Concessionaire	% to WCE	Total $ Revenue	$ to WCE (Gross)
204	Mosque of Tangiers	Jacob Benchetrit	25.0%	1,618	405
288	Cider, Midway	Mrs. W. R. Robeson	25.0%	2,633	658
300	Aztec Village	P. B. Mills	25.0%	10,233	2,558
253	Sitting Bull Log Cabin	P. B. Wickham	25.0%	10,564	2,641
221	Submarine Diving	J. J. Mannion & Co.	25.0%	18,030	4,507
238	Gold Mine	R. A. Campbell	25.0%	18,717	4,679
237	Panorama of Pompeii	G. Pandofelli	25.0%	19,506	4,876
248	American Indian Village	T. R. Roddy	25.0%	24,208	6,052
223	Ostrich Farm	A. J. Johnston	25.0%	44,826	11,206
257	Bedouin Camp	S. K. Bistanai	25.0%	47,218	11,804
177	New England Log Cabin	Mrs. E. S. Brinton	25.0%	51,553	12,888
133	Lapland Village	Lapland Village Exhibition Co.	25.0%	63,716	15,929
59	International Beauty Show	International Beauty Show Company	25.0%	166,021	41,508
13	Moorish Palace	Columbian Moorish Palace Co.	25.0%	449,048	112,356
25	Libbey Glass Co.	Libbey Glass Co.	25.0%	490,322	122,583
87	Hagenbeck Zoological Arena	Hagenbeck Zoolog. Arena Company	25.0%	526,709	131,174
322	East Indian Curios	Princess J. Sorabji	25.1%	11,631	2,923
31	Hungarian Café	Hungarian Café Co.	25.1%	50,611	12,684
326	Indian Curios	R. F. Hardy	25.2%	310	78
116	South Sea Island Theater	Oceanic Trading Co.	25.4%	93,224	23,647
39	World's Fair Captive Balloon Co.	World's Fair Captive Balloon Co.	25.6%	31,613	8,089
81	Vienna Café	Koenig & Greisser	26.2%	88,473	23,180
58	Ferris Wheel	George W. Ferris	28.9%	733,087	212,218
117	Model of the Eiffel Tower	C. du Pasquiere	29.9%	33,411	9,998
224	Java Village	Java-Chicago Exposition Co.	29.9%	154,895	46,300
86	St. Peter's Cathedral Model	Ludovic de Spiridon	33.2%	5,958	1,976
138	Tachyscopes	Arthur Schwartz	33.3%	4,553	1,518
324	Cider on the Plaisance	Davis & Whitman	33.3%	17,682	5,893
137	Electric Scenic Theater	Arthur Schwartz	33.3%	22,898	7,633
24	Volcano Mt. Kilauea	Lorrin A. Thurston	33.3%	61,561	20,496
14	Panorama Bernese Alps	Benjamin Henneberg	33.3%	64,233	21,407
48	Zoopraxigraphic Circus	Eadweard Muybridge	33.4%	320	107
61	Ice Railway	De La Vergne & Rankin	36.6%	67,319	24,665
69	Donegal Castle	Mrs. Alice M. Hart	42.5%	65,181	27,679
44	Diamond Match Co.	Diamond Match Co.	48.6%	804	391
43	Blarney Castle	Irish Industries Association	48.7%	138,869	67,658
1	Barre Sliding Railway	Barre Sliding RR Co. (*did not operate*)	—	—	—

Notes on the Financial Tables

Figures here for the Midway are complete and accurate with the exception that some concessions' claims for extraordinary expenses were allowed by the fair, essentially lowering the revenue paid to the fair. For the most part these were inconsequential. Only a portion of the concessions had any claims, and those that did were typically in the range of a few hundred to a few thousand dollars. The exceptions were the two Irish concessions—an interesting coincidence, as they were under different management. The two filed claims that were approved, reducing payments by a total of $68,588. Shown is the net due the fair *prior to deducting any claims* so that all concessions can be viewed similarly.

The claims filed and allowed could range from monies the concessions spent on improvements the fair requested, on mutual advertising, on losses experienced due to a problem related to the fair and not the concession, and so on. The details of claims were not disclosed in the final fair reports.

George Ferris made a variety of financial and contractual claims that ended in a legal battle that lasted long after the fair closed. Ferris claimed that his contract called for a reduction in commission paid to the fair for compensation of various construction expenses he incurred. When Ferris died in 1896 at just thirty-seven years of age, the claims were still unresolved.

Total Concession Revenue for the Fair

Total gross receipts for all of the WCE	$16,570,682	
Portion of all receipts as commission to the WCE	$4,237,564	
Total gross receipts for Midway concessions	$7,444,522	
Portion of Midway receipts as commission to the WCE	$1,672,761	(22.5%)
Total gross receipts for non-Midway concessions	$9,126,160	
Portion of non-Midway receipts as commission to the WCE	$2,564,803	(28.1%)

The Midway's fifty-four concessions (15 percent of the fair's total licensed concessions) generated 44.9 percent of all fair concession revenue and 39.8 percent of all commissions paid to the WCE.

Assuming, very roughly, that the current cost of living is twenty-five times what it was at the time of the fair, those Midway concessions with revenues of $40,000 or more had a contemporary equivalent of at least $1 million. Thus, thirty-two of the Midway concessions had sales of $1 million or more in current dollars. The highest-grossing concessions in current dollars were Cairo Street ($19.7 million) and the Ferris Wheel ($18.3 million), which operated for only four of the fair's six months.

Admissions to Midway Concessions

While fair management maintained detailed statistical data about the Midway, as with overall attendance, the purpose was solely to determine the amount that would accrue to the fair and ultimately retire its debt.

In Higinbotham's final report, he cited several interesting totals but did not provide any concession-by-concession data. The following admission figures reveal that the fair had some information differentiating revenue between admission to the site and admission to performances within each concession, but those details were never made available and are likely lost to history. But Higinbotham did summarize the number of fairgoers who paid to enter concessions:

Cairo Street	2,200,000
Hagenbeck's Arena	2,000,000
Ferris Wheel	1,500,000
German Village	800,000
Old Vienna	800,000
Java Village	670,000
Irish Industries	550,000

Notes on References and Sources

All publications cited and photographs used in this book are from my library, acquired over time beginning with my first discovery and interest in the World's Columbian Exposition in 1979.

As noted in the preface, several diaries and hundreds of personal letters and postcards were vital to the telling of the Midway's story. Excellent sources besides those listed here include many small and specialty guides from Conkey, which had the franchise to sell on the fairgrounds—overall guides, building guides, and topical guides. Also integral were dozens of guides and promotional booklets from Midway concessions, published either as giveaways or for sale at the fair for prices ranging from a nickel to a quarter. Today if one could find these booklets (virtually absent from the marketplace since the 1980s), most would fetch well over a hundred dollars each. Many of these, and probably most of the publications cited here, can be found in Chicago at the Public Library Special Collections, the Art Institute, and the Chicago Historical Society. Finally, nothing can replace the words, photos, impressions, and facts in the personal letters, cards, and diaries from during and immediately after the fair.

The serious researcher and student of the Columbian Exposition and the Midway will quickly recognize that hundreds—perhaps thousands—of photographs appeared repeatedly in different publications. Even captions from one book to another were often identical. A handful of professional photographers apparently sold their work to multiple publications; in other cases, the work of the fair's official photographer, C. D. Arnold, was provided to publications to help promote the fair. It is unlikely that an accurate count of Arnold photos and negatives exists, but he certainly must have taken ten thousand or more images. Again, Chicago institutions have vast holdings of his work. There are also many fine institutions throughout the county with extensive photographic and ephemera collections from the Columbian Exposition.

As noted in the acknowledgments, the people and the collections of the Art Institute of Chicago and Special Collections of the Chicago Public Library have been invaluable to me for more than two decades—and I highly recommend them for anyone serious about building a history of any aspect of the World's Columbian Exposition and the Midway Plaisance.

While it may be obvious, I would like to reiterate that eBay and other online sources, auctions, and used and antiquarian book dealers provide avenues to the many sources mentioned. As I built my own library of references and photographs used in the writing of this book, I discovered many rare resources inexpensively priced owing to detached covers or stained pages. The book may be drastically reduced in price—but the information is still invaluable.

Over the years researching the fair and this book, I have used literally thousands of sources. It would be impractical to list them all. I have listed a reasonable number of publications that provide the reader or researcher quality and comprehensive information and that can be found in many archives in Chicago, at university libraries, and at various collections throughout the country. Many libraries one would not expect to have Columbian material have outstanding collections primarily thanks to the generosity of a donor with some connection to Chicago and the fair.

Finally, by listing publications here I am not endorsing their infallibility. Virtually *every* Columbian Exposition publication from 1892 to 1894 contains some inaccuracies and questionable editorial subjectivity. That does not diminish their value, but it does put pressure on the reader not to make assumptions or to believe all the "facts" as they are offered. The reader must also exercise extreme diligence when not using primary research materials; as we all are aware, the Internet is an amazing source of information but is fraught with inaccuracies that are perpetuated by insufficient vetting of references.

Norm Bolotin

Books

The Art of the World Illustrated in the Paintings, Statuary and Architecture of the World's Columbian Exposition. Edition De Luxe. New York: D. Appleton and Company, 1893. In Five Volumes, Limited Edition of 1,000 copies (this copy being Number 808). Unnumbered pages.

Bancroft, Hubert. *The Book of the Fair and Columbian Exposition 1893: Historical and Descriptive Presentation of the World's Science, Art, and Industry, as viewed through the Columbian Exposition at Chicago in 1893.* Chicago and San Francisco: Bancroft Company, Publishers, 1893. 1,000 pages.

Bloom, Sol. *The Autobiography of Sol Bloom.* New York: G. P. Putnam's Sons, 1948. 345 pages.

Flinn, John J. *The Standard Guide to Chicago for the Year 1892.* N.p., 1892. Unnumbered pages.

Flinn, John J. *The Official Guide to the World's Columbian Exposition.* Chicago: The Columbian Guide Company, 1892. 301 pages.

Graham, Charles. *From Peristyle to Plaisance: World's Fair in Water Colors.* Chicago and Springfield, Ohio: Winters Art Lithography Company, 1893. Unnumbered pages.

The Graphic History of the Fair: The World's Columbian Exposition, Chicago 1893. Chicago: The Graphic Company, 1894. 240 pages.

Higinbotham, Harlow N. *Report of the President of the Board of Directors of the World's Columbian Exposition.* Chicago: Rand McNally and Company, 1898. Partially numbered pages.

The Historical World's Columbian Exposition 1893 and Chicago Guide. St. Louis and San Francisco: Pacific Publishing Company, 1892. Featuring the watercolors of Charles Graham. 500 pages.

Johnson, Rossiter. *A History of the World's Columbian Exposition Held in Chicago in 1893, by Authority of the Board of Directors.* New York: D. Appleton and Company, 1897. Four volumes, 2102 pages.

Photographs of the World's Fair: An Elaborate Collection of Photographs of the Buildings, Grounds and Exhibits of the World's Columbian Exposition. Chicago: Werner Company, 1894. 352 pages.

Portrait Types of the Midway: A Collection of Photographs of Individual Types of Various Nations from All Parts of the World. Introduction by F. W. Putnam, Harvard University and Chief of the Department of Ethnology at the World's Columbian Exposition. St. Louis: N. D. Thompson Publishing, 1894. Unnumbered pages.

Report of the Committee on Awards of the World's Columbian Commission. Washington, D.C.: Government Printing Office, 1901. Two volumes, 1694 pages.

Truman, Major Ben. *History of the World's Fair.* Chicago, 1893. 594 pages.

Truman, Major Ben. *History of the World's Fair.* Philadelphia: Mammoth Publishing Company, 1893. 610 pages.

A Week at the Fair, Illustrating the Exhibits and Wonders of the World's Columbian Exposition, Including Maps, Plans and Illustrations. [Chicago]: Rand, McNally and Company. 1893. Unnumbered pages.

White, Trumbull, and William Igleheart. *The World's Columbian Exposition 1893.* With contributions by Col. George Davis, Director General, and Mrs. Potter Palmer, President of the Board of Lady Managers of the World's Columbian Exposition. Boston: Standard Silverware Company, 1893. 628 pages.

The World's Fair and Midway Plaisance: The World's Fair in Picture and Story. Philadelphia: Manufacturers' Book Company, 1894. Unnumbered pages.

Periodicals

The Century Illustrated Monthly Magazine, The Century Company, New York, 1892–1893. Selected issues.

Chicago Tribune, 1891–1894. Selected issues.

*The Dream City: A Portfolio of Photographic Views of the World's Columbian Exposition, St. Louis, 1893. Selected issues.

*The Graphic, The Graphic Company, Chicago, 1892. Selected issues.

*Halligan's Illustrated World: A Portfolio of Photographic Views of the World's Columbian Exposition, Jewell N. Halligan Co., Chicago, New York, London, and Paris, 1893. Selected issues.

*The Magic City: A Portfolio of Original Photographic Views of the Great World's Fair and Its Treasures of Art, Including a Graphic Representation of the Famous Midway Plaisance, Historical Publishing Company, Philadelphia, 1892–1893. Selected issues.

North American Review, edited by Lloyd Bryce. New York, 1892. Selected issues.

*Picturesque World's Fair. William B. Conkey Publishers, Chicago, 1893. Selected issues.

*The White City as It Was: Educational Fine Art Series, The White City Art Company, Chicago and Denver, 1894. Selected issues.

**The World's Columbian Exposition Illustrated, Campbell's Publishing Company, Chicago, 1891–1893. Selected issues.

* These publications were all oversized portfolios (approximately 12 inches by 12 inches or larger) and published specifically for the fair. Their content consisted primarily of full-page photographs and detailed captions.

** Campbell's was a tabloid-size, heavily illustrated publication with both in-depth features and news articles and claimed a readership of 1.5 million at the height of fair interest.

Brochures and Guides Produced by Midway Concessions

The Javanese Theater, 5 × 7.75 inches, 22 pages, colored twine binding

Panorama of the Swiss Alps, 4.75 × 8 inches, 64 pages, staple bound

Hagenbeck's Arena, 6 × 9 inches, 8 pages, glue bound

Libbey Glass Company, 6 × 9 inches, 16 pages, staple bound

The Moorish Palace and its Startling Wonders, 6 × 8.75 inches, 16 pages

Cairo Street, 8.5 × 5 inches, 16 pages

Moorish Palace, 5 × 16 inches, broadside, single page

A Day in Germany, 4 × 8 inches, 8 pages

A Guide to the Tombs of THI and APIS, 8.5 × 5.5 inches, 4 pages

A Guide to the Egyptian Temple, 8.5 × 5.5 inches, 4 pages

African Ostriches, a ticket flyer handout, single sheet

Donegal Castle, 8.5 × 11, broadside, single page

Index

117

Norman Bolotin and Christine Laing manage The History Bank in Woodinville, Washington. Their books include *The World's Columbian Exposition: The Chicago World's Fair of 1893.*

The University of Illinois Press
is a founding member of the
Association of American University Presses.

Text designed by Jim Proefrock
Composed in 12/14 Adobe Caslon
with Monotype Grotesque display
at the University of Illinois Press
Cover designed by Dustin J. Hubbart
Cover illustration by Charles Graham
Manufactured by Sheridan Books, Inc.

University of Illinois Press
1325 South Oak Street
Champaign, IL 61820-6903
www.press.uillinois.edu